The Shire Horse

J. Albert Frost

Copyright © BiblioLife, LLC

This book represents a historical reproduction of a work originally published before 1923 that is part of a unique project which provides opportunities for readers, educators and researchers by bringing hard-to-find original publications back into print at reasonable prices. Because this and other works are culturally important, we have made them available as part of our commitment to protecting, preserving and promoting the world's literature. These books are in the "public domain" and were digitized and made available in cooperation with libraries, archives, and open source initiatives around the world dedicated to this important mission.

We believe that when we undertake the difficult task of re-creating these works as attractive, readable and affordable books, we further the goal of sharing these works with a global audience, and preserving a vanishing wealth of human knowledge.

Many historical books were originally published in small fonts, which can make them very difficult to read. Accordingly, in order to improve the reading experience of these books, we have created "enlarged print" versions of our books. Because of font size variation in the original books, some of these may not technically qualify as "large print" books, as that term is generally defined; however, we believe these versions provide an overall improved reading experience for many.

THE SHIRE HORSE
IN PEACE AND WAR

BY
J. ALBERT FROST

LONDON
VINTON & COMPANY, Ltd.
8, BREAM'S BUILDINGS, CHANCERY LANE, E.C.
1915

PREFACE

During the past year I have seen enquiries for a book on the management of Shire Horses; therefore I have made an attempt to supply the want. That the result leaves much—very much—to be desired I am well aware, but at least the little work is free from fine phrases and technical terms. Farmers prefer practical advice to literary merit in any book, or paper, that they read, and this is written by one of their own class.

For six months England has been engaged in war, the most awful yet waged for the reason that half the world is involved in it. It naturally follows that little is read but war news. Consequently these pages will be regarded as dull and uninteresting by those who have become accustomed to thrilling stories from battlefields, seas, or skies.

PREFACE

By those who take an interest in the world's heaviest breed of horses, as well as war news, this book may be tolerated, seeing that it deals with the old "War Horse" of Britain, many true descendants being actively engaged in moving "tons and guns" at the present time. I make no claim to having written anything new, but as a kind of pocket record of what Shire breeders, and exhibitors, have hitherto accomplished with their animals the facts herein contained may be useful, and I hope that all readers, as well as Shire breeders, will forgive any inaccuracies in my figures and all the imperfections in this my first attempt at book-writing.

In 1899 I won a small prize, offered by an agricultural paper for a short article entitled "Rent-Paying Horses," which I tried to point out were Shire Horses. Since then I have contributed a little to the live stock papers on the same subject, including an article for the *Farmer and Stockbreeder Year Book* of 1906, which is reprinted by the

PREFACE

editor's permission. It was over the initials "S. H. L.," which mean "Shire Horse Lover." I have been that from my school days, but never a greater one than now.

J. ALBERT FROST.

THE HOMESTEAD,
  BLETCHLEY, BUCKS.
    January, 1915.

For figures and quotations I am indebted to the Stud Books and Catalogues of the Shire Horse Society; the Journals of the Royal Agricultural Society of England; to articles on Shire Horses, in the *Live Stock Journal Almanac*, by the late Mr. G. M. Sexton (who died in 1894); and his successor, Mr. A. C. Beck; also to the late Sir Walter Gilbey's book on *The Great Horse*, published in 1899.

J. A. F.

CONTENTS

CHAPTER		PAGE
	AUTHOR'S PREFACE	v
I.	A POPULAR BREED	1
II.	FOUNDING A STUD	8
III.	THE SELECTION OF SIRES	12
IV.	BREEDING FROM FILLIES	17
V.	TEAM WORK	23
VI.	REARING AND FEEDING	30
VII.	CARE OF THE FEET	42
VIII.	HOW TO SHOW A SHIRE	48
IX.	ORIGIN AND PROGRESS OF THE SHIRE	51
X.	FACTS AND FIGURES	61
XI.	HIGH PRICES	69
XII.	A FEW RECORDS	76
XIII.	JUDGES AT THE LONDON SHIRE SHOWS, 1890–1915	87
XIV.	THE EXPORT TRADE	92
XV.	PROMINENT PRESENT-DAY STUDS	103
XVI.	THE FUTURE OUTLOOK	121
	INDEX	127

ILLUSTRATIONS

STALLION: CHAMPION'S GOALKEEPER . *Facing Title Page*
MARE: PAILTON SORAIS . *Facing Page* 1

THE SHIRE HORSE IN PEACE AND WAR

CHAPTER I

A Popular Breed

THERE is no breed of horses which has attracted so much attention during the past thirty years as the Old English War Horse. Originally bred and preserved for fighting purposes, his size was increased by importations of stallions and mares from Flanders—famous now and henceforth as the battleground of the greatest war ever waged. In the days when heavy armour was worn the cavalry horse could hardly be too stout, and at that time ploughing was performed by oxen; but there came a day when the English knights discarded their coats of mail and thenceforward sought for light-legged mounts. This gave the horses bred in "the Shires" a chance to distinguish themselves as draught horses, for which their width of chest, short legs, and strong back were well adapted: so the War Horse of the olden days became the Old English Cart Horse.

Farmers—particularly Robert Bakewell—discovered that they could do double, or treble, the quantity of ploughing with a pair of these heavy horses that they could with an ox team; therefore draught horses superseded bullocks for agricultural and haulage purposes, which meant that they were bred for weight and substance, the biggest and heaviest being regarded as the best.

Pedigrees of these massive animals were kept by a few progressive breeders from the year 1800, at least; therefore it was not difficult to compile a stud book for this Old English breed when a society, to protect its interests, and promote its breeding, was formed in 1878 by a body of admirers, among whom the late Sir Walter Gilbey was conspicuous. Included were also the Earl of Ellesmere, Earl Spencer, Lord Wantage, Lord Egerton of Tatton, the Hon. Edward Coke, Mr. Chandos Pole-Gell, Mr. Anthony Hamond, and Messrs. George and Frederic Street, while H.R.H. the Prince of Wales (King Edward VII) was a keen supporter of the Shire Horse Society from its inception.

All of those named have passed away; but not before they had seen their efforts bear rich fruit in the rapid establishment of the industry of Shire Horse breeding at home, and the world-wide fame achieved by the breed abroad, but particularly in the United States of America, to which country the majority of those exported have been sent.

Great changes have occurred since the Hon. E. Coke's dispersion sale at Longford Hall, Derby, in October, 1889, this being the first of which the writer possesses a catalogue. It was caused by his death, and his stud manager went from thence to take charge of the Royal Stud of Shires at Sandringham for King Edward, who proved to be a very successful breeder. Two champion mares, Gloaming and Solace, were bred, and more than one successful sale held at Sandringham in the 'nineties of last century, a decade during which it became the fashion for landowners and wealthy men to own a stud of Shires so that they almost tumbled over each other to secure the most notable specimens for their studs. (The last sale of King Edward's Shires was held at Wolferton in 1907.) The result was a reign of high prices which led many farmers to believe that Shire Horse breeding was beyond the reach of their pockets. Stud sales to the number of ten or twelve were held each year from 1890 to 1902, when the total was fourteen and the number of Shires sold 583, after which they began to dwindle till the past year of 1914, during which there was not a single home sale.

To an outsider this might be taken to prove that the love and enthusiasm for the Old English breed had fizzled out, that the Shire had been "weighed in the balances and found wanting." Nothing could be further from the truth. The last home sale held was the most successful that ever took place. Thirty-two animals, including several yearlings, averaged £454 each at Lord Rothschild's sale on February 14th, 1913, one two-year-old colt, Champion's Goalkeeper, making the record price for a Shire of 4,100 guineas. After this one may well wonder why such a good method of selling has been abandoned. The chief reason is that the industry is no longer confined to those who live in mansions, or think—financially—in thousands. It has become part of the routine of hundreds of English tenant farmers to rear Shire horses, and as they have only a few animals to offer at one time the Repository Sale has superseded the Home gathering, helpful though these fraternal meetings have always proved to the breed's interests.

As before stated, most of those who held sales have gone the way of all flesh, but besides those already named may be mentioned Sir P. A. Muntz, Lord Llangattock, Mr. John Parnell, Mr. Fred Crisp, Mr. Philo L. Mills, Mr. James Eadie, Mr. Arthur Ransom, and Mr. J. A. Barrs. All of these were buyers, breeders, and exhibitors of the best in their day, together with others too numerous to mention.

The loss of these supporters has, however, been made good by new ones, more numerous, if less influential; therefore the Shire breeding industry has never been on a broader base than it is to-day.

These lines are being written when horses

are in greater demand for war purposes than they have ever been before in the world's history, and although the Shire has for generations been transformed into a peace, rather than a war, horse he has not escaped the notice of the army buyer. We have it on the best authority—that of the official auctioneer to the Shire Horse Society—that "many a pure-bred Shire mare and gelding are now pulling heavy guns and transport waggons in France and Belgium, besides which nearly all the best gunners are by Shire stallions."

It is scarcely necessary to point out that the best Shires of this period weigh over one ton, and to pull weight you must have weighty animals; therefore these massive modern cart horses are just as useful in hauling heavy guns, the most effective weapons in modern warfare, as their ancestors were in carrying the bold British knights cased from head to foot in steel armour.

But war, though it lasts long—too long—comes to an end, and when this one does horses will be wanted in thousands to make up for those lost by the eight or nine nations now fighting for their existence.

It is perfectly clear that the great studs of Shires as they existed a few years ago are being dispersed. Very few breeders of the present time could have sixty high class animals paraded, as the late Lord Ellesmere did for the benefit of visitors to the Worsley show in August, 1889; but scores of farmers could muster a team or two of good Shire mares; therefore it is obvious that, whatever the future of the Shire may be, English farmers will do much towards shaping it.

CHAPTER II

FOUNDING A STUD

As this little book is intended for farmers more than for stud owners, a better heading for this chapter would have been "Selecting the Dams," for without sound, useful mares no breeder can hope to achieve success with the horses he breeds.

It has been possible to grade up one's old stock of mares by using registered stallions until they were eligible for the Stud Book; but this is too tedious a course to recommend in these days; moreover, the demand for draught mares is now so keen that the difference in the price of a pedigree and a common non-pedigree mare is scarcely worth considering. Therefore the beginner who wishes to breed pedigree Shires should dispose of his unregistered mares to re-invest his money in females which are worth mating with a really good sire, so that the full benefits of the industry may be more quickly forthcoming.

Of course there is a wide range of choice in Shire mares; consequently there is plenty of scope for the skill and judgment of the purchaser. Those which are fashionably bred, perfectly sound and likely to make prize winners usually realize high prices, while prizes already won add considerably to the market value of any Shire, male or female.

One must decide according to his means whether he will launch out and buy one or two of the most famous mares to be obtained, or whether he will proceed cautiously, and with as little outlay as possible, by picking up useful specimens as they come under his notice; but it may be pointed out that the man who attends sales and gives sensational prices advertises himself, thus getting a more favourable start than the plodder.

The initial, or foundation, stock, whatever its cost, should be free from hereditary unsoundness, otherwise disappointment will be encountered in the offspring.

It is much more easy to find sound Shires now than it was in the early years of the Shire

Horse Society, when the rejections for unsoundness were very numerous, as the following extract from a show report of the past will prove:—"The judges selected ten horses to be sent out for veterinary inspection in the hope, vain though it proved to be, that at least half of them would be again found in the ring with a certificate of soundness, so that no difficulty would be experienced in securing sufficient sound animals to which they could award the three prizes and the reserve number. Not so, however; and the stewards were compelled to seek in the boxes for other horses to be sent out for examination in order that the rosettes might be placed."

Unsoundness on such a scale has long ceased to exist, largely through the efforts of the Shire Horse Society in sticking to their rule of giving prizes and commendations to sound animals only.

This does not imply that unsoundness cannot be found in the Shires of to-day. Unfortunately it is still possible to buy a mare, or use a stallion, with undesirable and readily inherited complaints; therefore it is very necessary for farmers—who wish to make their

Shires do a share towards paying the rent—to discriminate between a sound and an unsound horse, or mare, or to decide for himself whether to take or refuse a blemished animal. There are many of the latter which often prove a good investment, and as a veterinary surgeon cannot always be found at a moment's notice it is desirable for breeders to make themselves acquainted with the conformation of a sound and perfectly moulded animal, so as to be able to rely on one's own judgment when buying or selling.

Shire Horse history has proved that the purchase of one sound mare with good back breeding has led to fame and fortune, a fact which should not be forgotten when home breeding is being embarked upon or extended.

CHAPTER III

THE SELECTION OF SIRES

THE question of mating is one of great importance in the breeding of any class of live stock, hence the necessity of rejecting a commonplace sire whether he is to be purchased or only patronized for nominations.

The cheap sire is common enough even in these days, and the fact that his services cost little gives him a popularity altogether unmerited and very injurious to the best interests of Shire breeding. Quite recently I saw twenty quarters of wheat delivered by a small farmer from whom it was purchased. In one of the carts I was surprised to find a five-year-old stallion, light in bone, pale chestnut in colour, and quite small—just the sort to haul guns or baggage to "the front" at the present time, but obviously unfit to serve a mare if a weighty cart horse was expected as the result. Yet the owner claimed to have got a lot of

THE SELECTION OF SIRES 13

mares to this horse for the past two seasons. This sort of thing going on all over the country, naturally lowers the standard. A farmer saves a yearling colt because he "likes the look of it." At two years old he uses him on his own mares and invites his neighbours to send theirs, the terms being something like £1 each mare, or, perhaps, "No colt, no pay," and £1 10s. if the mare proves to be in foal.

Such a system of breeding may help to increase the horse population, and those bred in this haphazard fashion may find a ready market while a great war is in progress, but it is not Shire breeding in the true sense; therefore a farmer who possesses even a useful mare should not object to paying a reasonable service fee, or, if he uses his neighbour's horse, he should at least ascertain if he is sound and of good parentage.

The work of the Shire Horse Society is to "improve the Old English Breed of Cart Horses." It has been carried on for thirty-six years very successfully, notwithstanding the injurious effect wrought by such stallions as that above mentioned, and it rests with the present members of the Shire Horse Society to carry on the work which, as aforesaid, was so well begun and maintained by such men as the late Sir Walter Gilbey, to whom all lovers of Shire Horses are indebted for his book on "The Great Horse," which gives the history of the breed from the time of the Roman Invasion till the year 1889 (when the first edition of the book appeared), at which date Shire Horse breeding had become a great national industry, that year having been the best on record for the number of export certificates granted. A second edition brings the work up to 1899.

When wealthy stud owners place the best of stallions within the reach of tenant farmers it is a mistake to miss the opportunity, but those less fortunately placed are now able, if they desire to do so, to profit by the Development Grant of the State, which enables them to get mares to sound—if not front rank—stallions at low fees or by assisted nominations. That a horse breeder should be content to mate his mares with a mongrel when it is easily possible to aim higher seems difficult to understand in these days when pedigree means so much in market value.

THE SELECTION OF SIRES

For the production of geldings, fashionable blood is not essential, but it sometimes happens that a foal of outstanding merit is bred by quite a small farmer, and if such an one is by a well-known sire of prize-winning stock, a real good price may be obtained, if the dam is only registered, so there is much to be said in favour of using the highest type of Shire stallion, even by owners of one or two mares. Fortunately farmers are able to secure special terms for their mares from most stud owners, and there are many local societies which hire a real good horse and charge a smaller sum to their own members than to outsiders. Among such societies may be mentioned Peterborough, Welshpool, and Winslow, in all of which districts many high-class Shires have been bred. Then there are generous landlords who hire a real good horse for the benefit of their tenants—although not Shire breeders themselves—so that it is quite possible for the majority of tenant farmers to obtain nominations to one of the best of Shire stallions if he is bent on improvement and believes in being enterprising enough to obtain it. The indifference which leads horse breeders to use a mongrel which comes into the yard, rather than send further afield to a better animal is inexcusable in a member of the Shire Horse Society, neither is such an one likely to improve his financial position by means of his heavy horses, which large numbers of farmers have done during the depressed times. An extra five pounds for a service fee may be, and often is, fifty when the foal is sold.

CHAPTER IV

BREEDING FROM FILLIES

FOR many years it has been a debatable point whether two-year-old fillies should be bred from or not. The pros and cons have been discussed, and in the end Shire breeders have used their own discretion on the point. Superior animals have, however, been bred from youthful parents on both sides, a notable instance being the late Lord Wantage's Lady Victoria; her sire was Prince William, the London and Royal Champion, and her dam Glow, by the London Champion Spark. She was the first foal of a two-year-old colt, with a two-year-old filly for her dam, yet she made a great prize-winning mare, having won first and cup in London in 1889 and championship of the Oxfordshire Show in 1890.

It may also be mentioned that Buscot Harold, the London Champion stallion of 1898, was begotten when his sire, Markeaton Royal

Harold, was but a two-year-old colt, although his dam, Aurea, was older. At two years old he was preferred to his sire for the Elsenham Challenge Cup.

This proves that Shire breeders have been making good use of fillies for many years, therefore the produce of a three-year-old filly need not be rejected, neither should the nursing of a foal at that age necessarily result in a stunted or plain mare. It is, however, necessary to grow fillies along with the aid of supplementary food and to "do" both them and their foals well while they are suckling.

There is no doubt that the Shires of the present day do get more food and attention than they did in bygone days, when it was unnecessary to strive after showyard size, because shows did not exist in such numbers, so that the farmer who exhibited cart horses was rarely met with, and young horse stock were not fed to encourage size and growth. So long as they could be put into the team at three years old and mated at four, that was considered early enough to work or to breed.

At the present time the horse population of Great Britain and Europe, if not of the whole

BREEDING FROM FILLIES

world, is being reduced by the greatest of all wars, consequently it is desirable for Shire breeders to do their share towards making good the shortage. If fillies are well kept from birth they will attain size and may be mated at two years old to a young horse, but not too early in the season. The end of May is early enough for fillies, and a big heavy old horse should not be chosen under any circumstances. If served at the right time they are more likely to breed than fillies a year older, and it makes a lot of difference whether a five-year-old mare has a couple of sons and daughters or even one to her credit, or no offspring at all, when the profit and loss account is being made up by a farmer.

It may be that a three-year-old cannot be got into a fat state for show with a foal running by her side, but the prolonged rest at that age does her no harm. She will come up all right at a later period, and is more likely to make a regular breeder than if not mated till three years old. A mare which breeds from the age of three till she is fifteen is a great help in the way of production, even if she only averages one foal in two years, which is, perhaps, as many as it is safe to reckon on for rearing to maturity, although, of course, there are plenty of mares which have produced a good foal for ten or eleven years in succession. They will breed till they are twenty-five, to the writer's knowledge, but the average age at which Shire mares breed their last foal must be put somewhere round fifteen.

There is no doubt that we have learned much in horse management since shows have become so popular, although it may be that high feeding for show purposes has been—and is—the cause of a lower percentage of foals among high class show animals of both sexes.

To prepare fillies for mating at two years old may be compared to feeding for early maturity in cattle and sheep, except that many of the latter are only grown and fattened to be killed, whereas Shires are meant to live a long and useful life. It is, therefore, necessary to build up a frame with this idea in view. An outdoor life should be led, while the food should be both good and sufficient, as well as being suitable.

There is no time to be wasted, and if foals are allowed to get into low condition while

BREEDING FROM FILLIES

being weaned, or during their first winter, they are less fit to make robust two-year-olds fit either to work or to breed, or what is more profitable, to accomplish both of these tasks together during part of the year.

If early maturity is aimed at with any class of stock, feeding and management must be of the best, therefore farmers who half starve their foals and allow their yearlings to be wintered on a bit of hay must not expect their two-year-olds to be well grown and in the best possible condition for parental duties.

The situation at the present time is such that every horse-breeder should do his best to utilize to the full the horse stock which he possesses, so that a sufficient number of horses may be obtained to carry on the agriculture and trade of the country, both of which are likely to require horses in large numbers in the immediate future.

Mares will be relatively more scarce than stallions for the reason that the latter have not been "commandeered" for war purposes, but as geldings have been taken in large numbers, there is, and will be, a great demand for workers of all grades.

Under such circumstances Shire breeders may serve their own interests by mating their fillies with a good young sire at two years old and keeping them in good condition for producing a strong vigorous foal. Very few of Robert Bakewell's remarks are recorded, but this one is, "The only way to be sure of good offspring is to have good cows as well as good bulls," and this applies with equal, if not greater, force in the business of horse-breeding; the sire cannot effect the whole of the improvement.

CHAPTER V

Team Work

SINCE my very youthful days I have always been accustomed to putting cart colts into the team at two years old, a system which cannot be too strongly advocated at the present time, when every worker in the shape of a horse is needed.

There are numbers of high-class Shires living a life of luxurious idleness to-day, for the only reason that they were never trained to work, yet they would be quite as well in health, and more likely to breed, if they were helping to do ploughing or almost any kind of farm work when not actually nursing a foal or being prepared for any important show.

When a Shire mare can be sold as "a good worker," a buyer feels that he is getting something for his money, even if she fails to breed, so that there is much to be said in favour of putting fillies into the team, and nothing against, so far as I know, unless they are over-worked, strained, or stunted.

A non-breeding mare which will not work is an impossible, or useless, sort of animal on a farm, where mere ornaments are not required, whereas if she is a worker in all gears she is "anybody's mare"; on the other hand, she is nobody's if she refuses either to work or to breed.

Geldings for haulage purposes are always in demand, but big powerful mares are equally useful for the same purpose, and it is much better to sell a non-breeder for the lorry than to sell her for another breeder to meet with disappointment. It is obvious that there will be a great scarcity of weighty working horses when the countries now involved in war settle down to peaceful trades and occupations, and there is no country which stands to benefit more than Great Britain, which is the best of all breeding grounds for draught horses.

To allow, what would otherwise be, a useful worker to eat the bread of idleness because it was regarded as too well bred or valuable to wear a collar is not a policy to pursue or to recommend, especially to farmers, seeing that the arable land tenant can put a colt into the team, between two steady horses at almost any time of the year, while the occupiers of grass farms may easily start their young Shires as workers by hitching them to a log of wood or some chain harrows, and afterwards work them in a roll.

There is no doubt, whatever, that many stallions would leave a much higher percentage of foals if they were "broken in" during their two-year-old days, so that they would take naturally to work when they grew older and could therefore be relied upon to work and thus keep down superfluous fat. This would be far better than allowing them to spend something like nine months of the year in a box or small paddock with nothing to do but eat.

In past times more working stallions could be found, and they were almost invariably good stock getters, but since showing has become popular it is almost a general rule to keep well-bred, or prize-winning, colts quite clear of the collar lest they should work themselves down in condition and so fail to please possible buyers on the look-out for show candidates.

A little more than twenty years ago there was an outcry against show condition in Shires, and this is what a very eminent breeder of those days said on the subject of fat—

"It is a matter of no consequence to any one, save their owners, when second or third-class horses are laden with blubber; but it is a national calamity when the best animals—those that ought to be the proud sires and dams of an ever-improving race—are stuffed with treacle and drugged with poisons in order to compete successfully with their inferiors. Hence come fever in the feet, diseased livers, fatty degeneration of the heart, and a host of ailments that often shorten the lives of their victims and always injure their constitutions."

This bears out my contention that Shires of both sexes would pay for a course of training in actual collar work, no matter how blue-blooded as regards ancestry or how promising for the show ring. The fact that a colt by a London champion had been seen in the plough team, or between a pair of shafts, would not detract from his value in the eyes of a judge, or prevent him from becoming a weighty and muscular horse; in fact, it would tend to the development of the arms and thighs which one expects to find in a Shire stallion, and if from any cause a stud or show career is closed, a useful one at honest work may still be carried on.

Wealthy stud owners can afford to pay grooms to exercise their horses, but farmers find—and are more than ever likely to find— that it is necessary to make the best possible use of their men; therefore, if their colts and fillies are put to work and rendered perfectly tractable, they will grow up as stallions which may be worked instead of being aimlessly exercised, while the mares can spend at least half of their lives in helping to carry on the ordinary work of the farm.

It is certainly worth while to take pains to train a young Shire, which is worth rearing at all, to lead from its foalhood days so that it is always approachable if required for show or sale, and these early lessons prepare it for the time when it is old enough to put its shoulders into the collar, this being done with far less risk than it is in the case of youngsters which have been turned away and neglected till they are three years old. The breaking in of this class of colt takes time and strength, while the task of getting a halter on is no light one, and the whole business of lungeing, handling, and harnessing requires more brute force and courage than the docile animal trained in infancy calls for.

The secret of training any horse is to keep it from knowing its own strength; therefore, if it is taught to lead before it is strong enough to break away, and to be tied up before it can break the headcollar by hanging back it is obvious that less force is required. The horse which finds he can break his halter by hanging back is likely to become a troublesome animal to stand tied up, while the one which throws its rider two or three times does not forget that it is possible to get a man off its back; therefore it is better and safer if they never gain such knowledge of their own powers.

The Shire breeding farmer ought to be able to go into his field and put a halter on any animal required, from a foal to an old horse, and he can do this if they have been treated with kindness and handled from their early days.

This is a matter to which many farmers

should give more attention than they do, seeing that an ill-trained show animal may lose a prize for no other reason than that its show manners are faulty, whereas those of the nearest rival are perfect.

The writer was taught this while showing at a County Show very early in his career. The animal he was leading was—like himself—rather badly educated, and this was noticed by one of the oldest and best judges of that day, and this is what he whispered in his ear, " My lad, if you would only spend your time training your horses instead of going to cricket they would do you more credit and win more prizes." This advice I have never forgotten, and I pass it on for the benefit of those who have yet to learn "the ropes."

CHAPTER VI

Rearing and Feeding

During the past few years we have heard much about early maturity with all kinds of stock. Four-year-old bullocks are rarely seen in these days, while wether sheep are being superseded by tegs. With Shire Horses there has been a considerable amount of attention paid to size in yearlings, two-and three-year-olds, which, as before stated, is equivalent to early maturity in the case of cattle and sheep. For the purpose of getting size an animal must be well fed from birth, and this applies to foals. Of course, the date of birth counts for a good deal when foals are shown with their dams, as it does to a less extent with yearlings, but after that age it makes very little difference whether a foal is born in February or in May.

From a farmer's point of view I do not believe in getting Shire foals too early. They have to be housed for a lengthened period, and the dams fed on food which may be expensive. At the present time good oats are worth 30s. per quarter, and hay, fit for horses, at least 90s. per ton, so that two or three months of winter feeding means a little sum added to the cost of raising a foal.

The middle of April is early enough for the average foal to arrive, and he can then make quite a good size by September if his dam is an ordinarily good suckler and he contracts no ailments, such as chills or scour, to check his progress. When colts are a month old they will begin to pick up crushed oats and bran while the dam is feeding, therefore it is no trouble to teach them to eat from a manger.

A word of caution is necessary to the inexperienced in the matter of feeding the dam until the foal is a few days old and strong enough to take all her milk. This is to feed the mare sparingly so as not to flush her milk while the youngster is unable to take it fast enough. Of course, the surplus can be milked away, as it should be if the bag is tight, but this may be neglected and then scour is often set up, which a very young foal often succumbs to. It is better that the mare should have too little than too much milk while the youngster gets fairly on his legs.

Cows always have most of their milk taken away, but young lambs as well as foals often suffer through taking too much of the dam's milk during the first day or two of their existence.

If a foal is born during the grazing season the flow of milk can be regulated by keeping the mare in a bare pasture, or shutting her up for part of the day.

Supposing that the foal survives the ills incidental to its early life, and gains in strength with the lengthening days, its first dry food will be taken when the mare is fed, which she should be, especially if she is either a young or an old mare, while show candidates will naturally need something more than grass. The object is to promote steady growth and maintain good health, and it should not be forgotten that oats are the best of all corn for horses; therefore no other kind should be given to a foal, but on good grazing land a mare will usually maintain herself and her

REARING AND FEEDING

foal in good condition for a good part of the summer without manger food.

It is towards weaning time that a manger is needed, into which should be put crushed (not whole) oats, together with an equal quantity of bran and a bit of good chaff. At the outset the mare will eat most of it, but the foal will benefit by getting richer milk and more of it, which he can now take without any ill effects. In time he acquires the habit of standing up to the manger and taking his share. It is very necessary to see that all foals eat well before they are weaned.

The cost of feeding a foal during its first winter may be roughly reckoned at ten shillings per week, which is made up as follows—

	s.	d.
80 lbs. of oats	6	0
56 „ hay	2	0
28 „ bran	1	6
28 „ oat straw	0	9
28 „ carrots	0	3

The bulk of the hay and all the oat straw should be fed in the form of chaff with the oats, bran and carrots (well cleaned and pulped), then a very good everyday diet can be formed by mixing the whole together, and one which few horses will refuse. Of course the items are not reckoned at the extreme prices prevailing in the winter of 1914–1915, but they could often be bought for less, so that it is a fair average.

It will be seen that oats form the biggest part, for the reason aforesaid, that they are better than other kinds of corn.

A little long hay should be given at night—more when there is snow on the ground—the other mixture divided into two feeds per day, morning and evening, unless showing is contemplated in the early Spring, when, of course, an extra feed will be given at mid-day.

The fashion has changed during the past few years as regards hay for horses. Meadow hay is regarded, and rightly so, as too soft, so hard seeds are invariably chosen by grooms or owners who want value for money.

It is quite easy to ascertain which a horse likes best by putting some good hard mixture and equally well-gotten meadow hay side by side in front of him. He will certainly eat that first which he likes best, and it will be found to be the harder mixture. The

REARING AND FEEDING

quantities mentioned are for foals which lie out or run on pasture.

The best place for wintering them is in a paddock or field, with a roomy shed open to the south. A yard, walled or slabbed on three sides, the south again being open to the field, with doors wide enough to admit a cart, is a very useful addition to the shed, as it is then possible to shut the youngsters in when necessary.

Both yard and shed should be kept littered, if straw is plentiful, but if not the shed should contain a good bedding of peat-moss litter. No overhead racks should be used, but one on the same level as the manger, so that no seeds drop out of the rack into the colt's eyes.

It will be found that foals reared in this way are healthy and ready for their feed, and they will often prefer to lie full length in the open than to rest in the shed. To see them lying quite flat and fast asleep, looking as if dead, is a pretty sure sign that they are thriving. They will often snore quite loudly, so that a novice may consider that they are ill.

Rock salt should be within reach for them to lick, together with good clean water. If a trough is used for the latter it should be cleaned out at intervals, and if a pond or ditch is the drinking place, there should be a stone mouth so as to avoid stalking in the mud. A healthy horse is a hungry horse, therefore the feed should be cleaned up before the next is put in. This must be noted in the case of foals just weaned. Any left over should be taken away and given to older horses, so that the little ones receive a sweet and palatable meal.

Condition and bloom may be obtained by adding a small quantity of boiled barley or a handful of linseed meal to the food above mentioned, while horses lying in should have a boiled linseed and bran mash about once a week.

It should be remembered, as before stated, that horses are not like cattle, sheep, or pigs, being fattened to be killed. They have a comparatively long life in front of them, so that it is necessary to build up a good constitution. Then they may change hands many times, and if they pass from where cooked foods and condiments are largely used to where plain food is given they are apt to refuse it and lose flesh in consequence, thus leading the new owner to suppose that he has got a bad bargain.

Reference has already been made to the pernicious system of stuffing show-animals, and it is not often that farmers err in this direction. They are usually satisfied with feeding their horses on sound and wholesome home-grown food without purchasing costly extras to make their horses into choice feeders.

It is always better for the breeder of any class of stock if the animals he sells give satisfaction to the purchasers, and this is particularly true of Shire horses. A doubtful breeder or one which is not all that it should be may be fattened up and sold at more than its market value, but the buyer would not be likely to go to the same man if he wanted another horse, therefore it is better to gain a reputation for honest dealing and to make every effort to keep it.

It might be here mentioned that it is not at all satisfactory to rear a Shire foal by itself, even if it will stay in its paddock. It never thrives as well as when with company, and often stands with its head down looking very mopish and dull, therefore the rearing of Shires is not a suitable undertaking for a small holder, although he may keep a good brood-mare to do most of his work and sell her foal at weaning time.

In the absence of a second foal a donkey is sometimes used as a companion to a single one, but he is a somewhat unsatisfactory playfellow, therefore the farmer with only one had far better sell it straight from the teat, or if he has suitable accommodation he should buy another to lie with it and rear the two together. Of course, two will need more food than one, but no more journeys will be required to carry it to the manger. Care should be taken, however, to buy one quite as good, and if possible better, than the home-bred one.

If they are to make geldings the colour should match, but if for breeding purposes the colour need not necessarily be the same. Except for making a working gelding, however, chestnuts should be avoided. It is not a desirable colour to propagate, so one can breed enough of that shade without buying one. A remark which may be also made with regard to unsound ones, viz. that most horse-breeders get enough of them without buying.

During their second summer—that is as yearlings—Shires not wanted for show purposes should be able to do themselves well at grass, supposing the land is of average quality and not overstocked, but if the soil is very poor it may be necessary to give a small feed once a day, of which pulped mangolds may form a part if they are plentiful. This extra feeding is better than stunting the growth, and the aim is to get a big romping two-year-old colt, filly, or gelding as the case may be.

Colts not up to the desired standard should be operated on during their yearling days, preferably in May or June, and, as before indicated, merit should be conspicuous in those left for stud purposes, while the back breeding on both sides counts for much in a stallion. That is why Lockinge Forest King, Childwick Champion, and a few others which could be named, proved to be such prepotent stock-getters.

After June or July colts should be separated from fillies unless the colts have been castrated, and they must be put inside good fences, this being something of a puzzle to a farmer with a few paddocks and poor fences. Consequently, a second or third-rate young stallion often causes a good deal of trouble, in fact, more than he leaves a return for.

For the second winter the young Shires still need a bit of help. If they are to make, or are likely to make, anything out of the common they should be fed liberally, otherwise a feed of chaff and corn once a day will do, with a bit of hay to munch at night, but it must be good wholesome forage.

During their second spring, or when two years old, they should be put to work as described in a former chapter, after which they are able at least to earn their keep; the cost of rearing on the lines indicated up to this age will be found to be considerable, so that a good saleable animal is needed to make the business a profitable one; but I have kept the rearing of good sound Shires in view, not crocks or mongrels.

The effect of the war on the cost of feeding horses has led the Board of Agriculture and Fisheries to issue a leaflet telling horse owners of substitutes for oats. When it was written beans were relatively cheaper, so was maize, while rice-meal was recommended to form part of the mixture, owing to its lower cost.

Those who have fed horses are aware that they do not like any food which is of a dusty nature. It sticks in their nostrils, causing them annoyance, if not discomfort, which a horse indicates by blowing its nose frequently.

Any kind of light meal should therefore be fed either with damp chaff or with pulped roots, well mixed with the feed in the manner described elsewhere. If mangolds have to be purchased at £1 per ton, they help to make the meals more palatable. The farmer who grows a variety of corn and roots is usually able to prepare and blend his own foods so as to make a diet on which horses will thrive although oats are scarce.

In Scotland boiled swedes or turnips are largely used for farm horses, but coal and labour are now scarce as well as horse corn.

CHAPTER VII

CARE OF THE FEET

THERE is no part of a Shire to which more attention should be paid than the feet, and it is safe to say that the foot of the present-day cart-horse is infinitely better than were those of his ancestors of forty, or even twenty, years ago. The shape as well as the size has been improved till the donkey-shaped hoof is rarely met with, at least in show animals of this breed.

It is always advisable to keep the feet of foals, yearlings, and two-year-olds attended to whether they are required for show or not, and if they have their feet quietly picked up and the edges rasped, the heels being lowered a little when necessary, the hoof is prevented from breaking, and a better and more durable hoof well repays the trouble, moreover the task of fixing the first set of shoes—which used to be quite a tough job for the smith

CARE OF THE FEET

when the colts were neglected till they were three years old—is rendered quite easy.

Except for travelling on the road, or when required for show, there is no advantage in keeping shoes on young Shires, therefore they should be taken off when lying idle, or if worked only on soft ground shoes are not actually necessary.

Where several are lying together, or even two, those with shoes on may cause ugly wounds on their fellows, whereas a kick with the naked hoof is not often serious. There is also a possibility that colts turned away to grass with their shoes on will have the removing neglected, and thus get corns, so that the shoeless hoof is always better for young Shires so long as it is sound and normal. If not, of course, it should be treated accordingly.

In a dry summer, when the ground is very hard, it may be advisable to use tips so that the foot may be preserved, this being especially necessary in the case of thin and brittle hoofs.

For growing and preserving good strong feet in Shire horses clay land seems to answer best, seeing that those reared on heavy-land farms almost invariably possess tough horn on which a shoe can be affixed to last till it wears out.

For the purpose of improving weak feet in young Shires turning them out in cool clay land may be recommended, taking care to assist the growth by keeping the heels open so that the frog comes into contact with the ground.

Weakness in the feet has been regarded, and rightly so, as a bad fault in a Shire stallion, therefore good judges have always been particular to put bottoms first when judging. Horses of all kinds have to travel, which they cannot do satisfactorily for any length of time if their feet are ill-formed or diseased, and it should be borne in mind that a good or a bad foot can be inherited. "No foot, no horse," is an old and true belief. During the past few years farmers have certainly paid more attention to the feet of their young stock because more of them are shown, the remarks of judges and critics having taught them that a good top cannot atone for poor bottoms, seeing that Shires are not like stationary

CARE OF THE FEET

engines, made to do their work standing. They have to spend a good part of their lives on hard roads or paved streets, where contracted or tender feet quickly come to grief, therefore those who want to produce saleable Shires should select parents with the approved type of pedals, and see that those of the offspring do not go wrong through neglect or mismanagement.

There is no doubt that a set of good feet often places an otherwise moderate Shire above one which has other good points but lacks this essential; therefore all breeders of Shires should devote time and attention to the production of sound and saleable bottoms, remembering the oft-quoted line, " The top may come, the bottom never." In diseases of the feet it is those in front which are the most certain to go wrong, and it is these which judges and buyers notice more particularly.

If fever manifests itself it is generally in the fore feet; while side-bone, ring-bone, and the like are incidental to the front coronets.

Clay land has been spoken of for rearing Shires, but there are various kinds of soil in England, all of which can be utilized as a breeding ground for the Old English type of cart-horses.

In Warwickshire Shires are bred on free-working red land, in Herts a chalky soil prevails, yet champions abound there; while very light sandy farms are capable of producing high-class Shires if the farmer thereof sets his mind on getting them, and makes up for the poorness or unsuitability of the soil by judicious feeding and careful management.

It may be here stated that an arable farm can be made to produce a good deal more horse forage than one composed wholly of pasture-land, therefore more horses can be kept on the former.

Heavy crops of clovers, mixtures, lucerne, etc., can be grown and mown twice in the season, whereas grass can only be cut once. Oats and oat straw are necessary, or at least desirable, for the rearing of horses, so are carrots, golden tankard, mangold, etc.; consequently an arable-land farmer may certainly be a Shire horse breeder.

This is getting away from the subject of feet, however, and it may be returned to by saying that stable management counts for a good deal in the growth and maintenance of a sound and healthy hoof.

Good floors kept clean, dry litter, a diet in which roots appear, moving shoes at regular intervals, fitting them to the feet, and not rasping the hoof down to fit a too narrow shoe, may be mentioned as aids in retaining good feet.

As stated, the improvement in this particular has been very noticeable since the writer's first Shire Horse Show (in 1890), but perfection has not yet been reached, therefore it remains for the breeders of the present and the future to strive after it.

There was a time when exhibitors of "Agricultural" horses stopped the cracks and crevices in their horses' feet with something in the nature of putty, which is proved by reading a report of the Leeds Royal of 1861, where "the judges discovered the feet of one of the heavy horses to be stopped with gutta-percha and pitch."

CHAPTER VIII

How to Show a Shire

A FEW remarks on the above subject will not come amiss, at least to the uninitiated, for it is tolerably certain that, other things being equal, the candidate for honours which makes the best show when it is actually before the judges stands the first chance of securing the honours.

It must not be expected that a colt can be fetched out of a grass field one day and trained well enough to show himself off creditably in the ring the next; and a rough raw colt makes both itself and its groom look small. Training properly takes time and patience, and it is best to begin early with the process, from birth for choice. The lessons need not, and certainly should not, be either long or severe at the outset, but just enough to teach the youngster what is required of him. When teaching horses to stand at "attention" they should not be made to stretch themselves out as if they were wanted to reach from one side of the ring to the other, neither should they be allowed to stand like an elephant on a tub. They should be taught to stand squarely on all fours in a becoming and businesslike way. The best place for the groom when a horse is wanted to stand still is exactly in front and facing the animal. The rein is usually gripped about a foot from the head. Mares can often be allowed a little more "head," but with stallions it may be better to take hold close to the bit, always remembering to have the loop end of the rein in the palm, in case he suddenly rears or plunges. The leader should "go with his horse," or keep step with him, but need not "pick up" in such a manner as to make it appear to bystanders that he is trying to make up for the shortcomings of his horse.

Both horse and man want to practise the performance in the home paddock a good many times before perfection can be reached, and certainly a little time thus spent is better than making a bad show when the critical moment arrives that they are both called out to exhibit themselves before a crowd of critics.

If well trained the horse will respond to the call of the judges with only a word, and no whip or stick need be used to get it through the required walks and trots, or back to its place in the rank.

There is a class of men who would profit by giving a little time to training young horse stock, and that is the farmers who breed but do not show. Of course, "professional showmen" (as they are sometimes called) prefer to "buy their gems in the rough," and put on the polish themselves, and then take the profits for so doing. But why should not the breeder make his animals show to their very best, and so get a better price into his own pocket?

Finally, I would respectfully suggest that if some of the horse show societies were to have a horse-showing competition, *i.e.* give prizes to the men who showed out a horse in the best manner, it would be both interesting and instructive to horse lovers.

CHAPTER IX

Origin and Progress of the Shire

It is evident that a breed of comparatively heavy horses existed in Britain at the time of the Roman Invasion, when Queen Boadicea's warriors met Cæsar's fighting men (who were on foot) in war chariots drawn by active but powerful horses, remarkable—as Sir Walter Gilbey's book on "The Great Horse" says—for "strength, substance, courage and docility."

These characteristics have been retained and improved upon all down the ages since. The chariot with its knives, or blades, to mow down the enemy was superseded by regiments of cavalry, the animals ridden being the Old English type of War Horse. In those days it was the lighter or second-rate animals, what we may call "the culls," which were left for agricultural purposes. The English knight, when clad in armour, weighed something like 4 cwt., therefore a weedy animal would have sunk under such a burden.

This evidently forced the early breeders to avoid long backs by breeding from strong-loined, deep-ribbed and well coupled animals, seeing that slackness meant weakness and, therefore, worthlessness for war purposes.

It is easy to understand that a long-backed, light-middled mount with a weight of 4 cwt. on his back would simply double up when stopped suddenly by the rider to swing his battle axe at the head of his antagonist, so we find from pictures and plates that the War Horse of those far-off days was wide and muscular in his build, very full in his thighs, while the saddle in use reached almost from the withers to the hips, thus proving that the back was short.

There came a time, however, when speed and mobility were preferred to mere weight. The knight cast away his armour and selected a lighter and fleeter mount than the War Horse of the ancient Britons.

The change was, perhaps, began at the battle of Bannockburn in 1314. It is recorded that Robert Bruce rode a "palfrey" in that battle, on which he dodged the charges of the ponderous English knights, and he took a very heavy toll, not only of English warriors but of their massive horses; therefore it is not unreasonable to suppose that some of the latter were used for breeding purposes, and thus helped to build up the Scottish, or Clydesdale, breed of heavy horses; but what was England's loss became Scotland's gain, in that the Clydesdale breed had a class devoted to it at the Highland Society's Show in 1823, whereas his English relative, "the Shire," did not receive recognition by the Royal Agricultural Society of England till 1883, sixty years later. As a War Horse the British breed known as "The Great Horse" seems to have been at its best between the Norman Conquest, 1066, and the date of Bannockburn above-mentioned, owing to the fact that the Norman nobles, who came over with William the Conqueror, fought on horseback, whereas the Britons of old used to dismount out of their chariots, and fight on foot. The Battle of Hastings was waged between Harold's English Army of infantrymen and William the Conqueror's Army of horsemen, ending in a victory for the latter.

The Flemish horses thus became known to

English horse breeders, and they were certainly used to help lay the foundation of the Old English breed of cart horses.

It is clear that horses with substance were used for drawing chariots at the Roman invasion in the year 55 B.C., but no great development in horse-breeding took place in England till the Normans proved that warriors could fight more effectively on horseback than on foot. After this the noblemen of England appear to have set store by their horses, consequently the twelfth and thirteenth centuries may be regarded as the age in which Britain's breed of heavy horses became firmly established.

In Sir Walter Gilbey's book is a quotation showing that "Cart Horses fit for the dray, the plough, or the chariot" were on sale at Smithfield (London) every Friday, the extract being made from a book written about 1154, and from the same source we learn that during the reign of King John, 1199–1216, a hundred stallions "of large stature" were imported from the low countries—Flanders and Holland.

Passing from this large importation to the time of the famous Robert Bakewell of Dishley (1726–1795), we find that he too went to

Flanders for stock to improve his cart horses, but instead of returning with stallions he bought mares, which he mated with his stallions, these being of the old black breed peculiar—in those days—to Leicestershire. There is no doubt that the interest taken by this great breed improver in the Old English type of cart horse had an effect far more important than it did in the case of the Longhorn breed of cattle, seeing that this has long lost its popularity, whereas that of the Shire horse has been growing and widening from that day to this.

Bakewell was the first English stockbreeder to let his stud animals for the season, and although his greatest success was achieved with the Dishley or "New Leicester" sheep, he also carried on the system with Longhorn bulls and his cart horses, which were described as "Bakewell's Blacks."

That his horses had a reputation is proved by the fact that in 1785 he had the honour of exhibiting a black horse before King George III. at St. James's Palace, but another horse named "K," said by Marshall to have died in that same year, 1785, at the age of nineteen years, was described by the writer just quoted as a better animal than that inspected by His Majesty the King. From the description given he appears to have had a commanding forehand and to have carried his head so high that his ears stood perpendicularly over his fore feet, as Bakewell held that the head of a cart horse should. It can hardly be questioned that he was a believer in weight, seeing that his horses were "thick and short in body, on very short legs."

The highest price he is credited with getting for the hire of a stallion for a season is 150 guineas, while the service fee at home is said to have been five guineas, which looks a small amount compared with the 800 guineas obtained for the use of his ram "Two Pounder" for a season."

What is of more importance to Shire horse breeders, however, is the fact that Robert Bakewell not only improved and popularized the Shire horse of his day, but he instituted the system of letting out sires for the season, which has been the means of placing good sires before farmers, thus enabling them to assist in the improvement which has made such strides

PROGRESS OF THE SHIRE

since the formation of the Shire Horse Society in 1878.

It is worth while to note that Bakewell's horses were said to be "perfectly gentle, willing workers, and of great power." He held that bad pullers were made so by bad management. He used two in front of a Rotherham plough, the quantity ploughed being "four acres a day." Surely a splendid advertisement for the Shire as a plough horse.

Flemish Blood

In view of the fact that Flanders has been very much in the public eye for the past few months owing to its having been converted into a vast battlefield, it is interesting to remember that we English farmers of to-day owe at least something of the size, substance and soundness of our Shire horses to the Flemish horse breeders of bygone days. Bakewell is known to have obtained marvellous results among his cattle and sheep by means of in-breeding, therefore we may assume that he would not have gone to the Continent for an outcross for his horses unless he regarded such a step beneficial to the breed.

It is recorded by George Culley that a certain Earl of Huntingdon had returned from the Low Countries—where he had been Ambassador—with a set of black coach horses, mostly stallions. These were used by the Trentside farmers, and without a doubt so impressed Bakewell as to induce him to pay a visit to the country whence they came.

If we turn from the history of the Shire to that of the Clydesdale it will be found that the imported Flemish stallions are credited by the most eminent authorities, with adding size to the North British breed of draught horses.

The Dukes of Hamilton were conspicuous for their interest in horse breeding. One was said to have imported six black Flemish stallions—to cross with the native mares—towards the close of the seventeenth century, while the sixth duke, who died in 1758, imported one, which he named "Clyde."

This is notable, because it proves that both the English and Scotch breeds have obtained size from the very country now devastated by war.

It may be here mentioned that one of the greatest lovers and breeders of heavy horses during the nineteenth century was schooled on the Duke of Hamilton's estate, and he was eminently successful in blending the Shire and Clydesdale breeds to produce prizewinners and sires which have done much towards building up the modern Clydesdale.

This was Mr. Lawrence Drew, of Merryton, who, like Mr. Robert Bakewell, had the distinction of exhibiting a stallion (named Prince of Wales) before Royalty.

It is well known that he (Mr. Drew) bought many Shires in the Midland Counties of England. So keen was his judgment that he would "spot a winner" from a railway carriage, and has been known to alight at the next station and make the journey back to the farm where he saw the likely animal.

On at least one occasion the farmer would not sell the best by itself, so the enthusiast bought the whole team, which he had seen at plough from the carriage window on the railway.

Quite the most celebrated Shire stallion purchased by Mr. Drew in England was Lincolnshire Lad 1196, who died in his possession in 1878. This horse won several prizes in Derbyshire before going north, and he also begot Lincolnshire Lad II. 1365, the sire of Harold 3703, Champion of the London Show of 1887, who in turn begot Rokeby Harold (Champion in London as a yearling, a three-year-old and a four-year-old), Markeaton Royal Harold, the Champion of 1897, and of Queen of the Shires, the Champion mare of the same year, 1897, and numerous other celebrities. A great mare, bought by Mr. Drew in Derbyshire, was Flora, by Lincolnshire Lad, who became the dam of Pandora, a great winner, and the dam of Prince of Clay, Handsome Prince, and Pandora's Prince, all of which were Clydesdale stallions and stock-getters of the first rank.

There is evidence to show that heavy horses from other countries than Flanders were imported, but this much is perfectly clear, that the Flemish breed was selected to impart size, therefore, if we give honour where it is due, these "big and handsome" black stallions that we read of deserve credit for helping to build up the breed of draught horses in Britain, which is universally known as the Shire, its distinguishing feature being that it is the heaviest breed in existence.

CHAPTER X

FACTS AND FIGURES

THE London Show of 1890 was a remarkable one in more than one sense. The entries totalled 646 against 447 the previous year. This led to the adoption of measures to prevent exhibitors from making more than two entries in one class. The year 1889 holds the record, so far, for the number of export certificates granted by the Shire Horse Society, the total being 1264 against 346 in 1913, yet Shires were much dearer in the latter year than in the former.

Twenty-five years ago the number of three-year-old stallions shown in London was 161, while two-year-olds totalled 134, hence the rule of charging double fees for more than two entries from one exhibitor.

Another innovation was the passing of a rule that every animal entered for show should be passed by a veterinary surgeon, this being the form of certificate drawn up :—

"I hereby certify that   entered by Mr.   for exhibition at the Shire Horse Society's London Show, 1891, has been examined by me and, in my opinion, is free from the following hereditary diseases, viz : Roaring (whistling), Ringbone, Unsound Feet, Navicular Disease, Spavin, Cataract, Sidebone, Shivering."

These alterations led to a smaller show in 1891 (which was the first at which the writer had the honour of leading round a candidate, exhibited by a gentleman who subsequently bred several London winners, and who served on the Council of the Shire Horse Society). But to hark back to the 1890 Show. The Champion Stallion was Mr. A. B. Freeman-Mitford's (now Lord Redesdale) Hitchin Conqueror, one of whose sons, I'm the Sort the Second, made £1000 at the show after winning third prize; the second-prize colt in the same class being sold for £700.

The Champion mare was Starlight, then owned by Mr. R. N. Sutton-Nelthorpe, but

FACTS AND FIGURES

sold before the 1891 Show, at the Scawby sale, for 925 guineas to Mr. Fred Crisp—who held a prominent place in the Shire Horse world for several years. Starlight rewarded him by winning Champion prize both in 1891 and 1892, her three successive victories being a record in championships for females at the London Show. Others have won highest honours thrice, but, so far, not in successive years.

In 1890 the number of members of the Shire Horse Society was 1615, the amount given in prizes being just over £700. A curious thing about that 1890 meeting, with its great entry, was that it resulted in a loss of £1300 to the Society, but in those days farmers did not attend in their thousands as they do now.

The sum spent in 1914 was £2230, the number of members being 4200, and the entries totalling 719, a similar sum being offered, at the time this is being written, for distribution at the Shire Horse Show of 1915, which will be held when this country has, with the help of her Allies, waged a great war for seven months, yet before it had been carried on for seven days show committees in various parts of the country cancelled their shows, being evidently under the impression that "all was in the dust." With horses of all grades at a premium, any method of directing the attention of farmers and breeders generally to the scarcity that is certain to exist is justifiable, particularly that which provides for over two thousand pounds being spent among members of what is admitted to be the most flourishing breed society in existence.

At the London Show of 1895 two classes for geldings were added to the prize schedule, making fifteen in all, but even with twenty-two geldings the total was only 489, so that it was a small show, its most notable feature being that Mr. A. B. Freeman-Mitford's Minnehaha won the Challenge Cup for mares and died later.

Up till the Show of 1898 both stallions and mares commenced with the eldest, so that Class I was for stallions ten years old and upwards, the yearlings coming last, the mare classes following in like order. But for the 1898 Show a desirable change was made by putting the yearlings first, and following on with classes in the order of age. At this show, 1898, Sir Alexander Henderson performed the unique feat of winning not only the male and female Challenge Cups, but also the other two, so that he had four cup winners, three of them being sire, dam, and son, viz. Markeaton Royal Harold, Aurea, and Buscot Harold, this made the victory particularly noteworthy. The last named also succeeded in winning champion honours in 1899 and 1900, thus rivalling Starlight. The cup-winning gelding, Bardon Extraordinary, had won similar honours the previous year for Mr. W. T. Everard, his owner in 1898 being Mr. James Eadie. He possessed both weight and quality, and it is doubtful if a better gelding has been exhibited since. He was also cup winner again in 1899, consequently he holds the record for geldings at the London Show.

It should have been mentioned that the system of giving breeders prizes was introduced at the Show of 1896, the first prizes being reduced from £25 to £20 in the case of stallions, and from £20 to £15 in those for mares, to allow the breeder of the first prize animal £10 in each breeding class, and the breeder of each second-prize stallion or mare £5, the latter sum being awarded to breeders of first-prize geldings. This was a move in the right direction, and certainly gave the Shire Horse Society and its London Show a lift up in the eyes of farmers who had bred Shires but had not exhibited. Since then they have never lost their claim on any good animal they have bred, that is why they flock to the Show in February from all parts of England, and follow the judging with such keen interest; there is money in it.

This Show of 1896 was, therefore, one of the most important ever held. It marked the beginning of a more democratic era in the history of the Great Horse. The sum of £1142 was well spent.

By the year 1900 the prize money had reached a total of £1322, the classes remaining as from 1895 with seven for stallions, six for mares, and two for geldings. The next year, 1901, another class, for mares 16 hands 2 inches and over, was added, and also another class for geldings, resulting in a further rise to £1537 in prize money. The sensation of this Show was the winning of the Championship by new tenant-farmer exhibitors, Messrs. J. and M. Walwyn, with an unknown two-year-old colt, Bearwardcote Blaze. This was a bigger surprise than the success of Rokeby Harold as a yearling in 1893, as he had won prizes for his breeder, Mr. A. C. Rogers, and for Mr. John Parnell (at Ashbourne) before getting into Lord Belper's possession, therefore great things were expected of him, whereas the colt Bearwardcote Blaze was a veritable "dark horse." Captain Heaton, of Worsley, was one of the judges, and subsequently purchased him for Lord Ellesmere.

The winning of the Championship by a yearling colt was much commented on at the time (1893), but he was altogether an extraordinary colt. The critics of that day regarded him as the best yearling Shire ever seen. Said one, "We breed Shire horses every day, but a colt like this comes only once in a lifetime." Fortunately I saw him both in London and at the Chester Royal, where he was also Champion, my interest being all the greater because he was bred in Bucks, close to where I "sung my first song."

Of two-year-old champions there have been at least four, viz. Prince William, in 1885; Buscot Harold, 1898; Bearwardcote Blaze, 1901; and Champion's Goalkeeper, 1913.

Three-year-olds have also won supreme honours fairly often. Those within the writer's recollection being Bury Victor Chief, in 1892, after being first in his class for the two previous years, and reserve champion in 1891; Rokeby Harold in 1895, who was Champion in 1893, and cup winner in 1894; Buscot Harold, in 1899, thus repeating his two-year-old performance; Halstead Royal Duke in 1909, the Royal Champion as a two-year-old.

The 1909 Show was remarkable for the successes of Lord Rothschild, who after winning one of the championships for the previous six years, now took both of the Challenge Cups, the reserve championship, and the Cup for the best old stallion.

The next and last three-year-old to win was, or is, the renowned Champion's Goalkeeper, who took the Challenge Cup in 1914 for the second time.

When comparing the ages of the male and female champions of the London Show, it is seen that while the former often reach the pinnacle of fame in their youth, the latter rarely do till they have had time to develop.

CHAPTER XI

HIGH PRICES

IT is not possible to give particulars of sums paid for many animals sold privately, as the amount is often kept secret, but a few may be mentioned. The first purchase to attract great attention was that of Prince William, by the late Lord Wantage from Mr. John Rowell in 1885 for £1500, or guineas, although Sir Walter Gilbey had before that given a real good price to Mr. W. R. Rowland for the Bucks-bred Spark. The next sensational private sale was that of Bury Victor Chief, the Royal Champion of 1891, to Mr. Joseph Wainwright, the seller again being Mr. John Rowell and the price 2500 guineas. In that same year, 1891, Chancellor, one of Premier's noted sons, made 1100 guineas at Mr. A. C. Duncombe's sale at Calwich, when eighteen of Premier's sons and daughters were paraded with their sire, and made an average, including foals, of £273 each.

In 1892 a record in letting was set up by the Welshpool Shire Horse Society, who gave Lord Ellesmere £1000 for the use of Vulcan (the champion of the 1891 London Show) to serve 100 mares. This society was said to be composed of "shrewd tenant farmers who expected a good return for their money." Since then a thousand pounds for a first-class sire has been paid many times, and it is in districts where they have been used that those in search of the best go for their foals. Two notable instances can be mentioned, viz. Champion's Goalkeeper and Lorna Doone, the male and female champions of the London Show of 1914, which were both bred in the Welshpool district. Other high-priced stallions to be sold by auction in the nineties were Marmion to Mr. Fred Crisp from Mr. Arkwright in 1892 for 1400 guineas, Waresley Premier Duke to Mr. Victor Cavendish (now the Duke of Devonshire) for 1100 guineas at Mr. W. H. O. Duncombe's sale in 1897, and a similar sum by the same buyer for Lord Llangattock's Hendre Crown Prince in the same year.

HIGH PRICES

For the next really high-priced stallion we must come to the dispersion of the late Lord Egerton's stud in April, 1909, when Messrs. W. and H. Whitley purchased the five-year-old Tatton Dray King (London Champion in 1908) for 3700 guineas, to join their celebrated Devonshire stud. At this sale Tatton Herald, a two-year-old colt, made 1200 guineas to Messrs. Ainscough, who won the championship with him at the Liverpool Royal in 1910, but at the Royal Show of 1914 he figured, and won, as a gelding.

As a general rule, however, these costly sires have proved well worth their money.

As mentioned previously, the year 1913 will be remembered by the fact that 4100 guineas was given at Lord Rothschild's sale for the two-year-old Shire colt Champion's Goalkeeper, by Childwick Champion, who, like Tatton Dray King and others, is likely to prove a good investment at his cost. Twice since then he has championed the London Show, and by the time these lines are read he may have accomplished that great feat for the third time, his age being four years old in 1915.

Of mares, Starlight, previously mentioned, was the first to approach a thousand pounds in an auction sale.

At the Shire Horse Show of 1893 the late Mr. Philo Mills exhibited Moonlight, a mare which he had purchased privately for £1000, but she only succeeded in getting a commended card, so good was the company in which she found herself. The first Shire mare to make over a thousand guineas at a stud sale was Dunsmore Gloaming, by Harold. This was at the second Dunsmore Sale early in 1894, the price being 1010 guineas, and the purchaser Mr. W. J. Buckley, Penyfai, Carmarthen, from whom she was repurchased by the late Sir P. Albert Muntz, and was again included in the Dunsmore catalogue of January 27, 1898, when she realized 780 guineas, Sir J. Blundell Maple being the lucky purchaser, the word being used because she won the challenge cup in London, both in 1899 and 1900. Foaled in 1890 at Sandringham, by Harold (London Champion), dam by Staunton Hero (London Champion), she was sold at King Edward's first sale in 1892 for 200 guineas. As a three- and a four-year-old she

HIGH PRICES

was second in London, and she also won second prize as a seven-year-old for Sir P. A. Muntz, finally winning supreme honours at nine and ten years of age, a very successful finish to a distinguished career. On February 11th, 1898, another record was set by His Majesty King Edward VII., whose three-year-old filly Sea Breeze, by the same sire as Beardwardcote Blaze, made 1150 guineas, Sir J. Blundell Maple again being the buyer. The next mare to make four figures at a stud sale was Hendre Crown Princess at the Lockinge sale of February 14, 1900, the successful bidder being Mr. H. H. Smith-Carington, Ashby Folville, Melton Mowbray, who has bought and bred many good Shires. The price was 1100 guineas. This date, February 14, seems to be a particularly lucky one for Shire sales, for besides the one just mentioned Lord Rothschild has held at least two sales on February 14. In 1908 the yearling colt King Cole VII. was bought by the late Lord Winterstoke for 900 guineas, the highest price realized by the stud sales of that year. Then there is the record sale at Tring Park on February 14, 1913, when one stallion, Champions

Goalkeeper, made 4100 guineas, and another, Blacklands Kingmaker, 1750.

The honour for being the highest priced Shire mare sold at a stud sale belongs to the great show mare, Pailton Sorais, for which Sir Arthur Nicholson gave 1200 guineas at the dispersion sale of Mr. Max Michaelis at Tandridge, Surrey, on October 26, 1911. It will be remembered by Shire breeders that she made a successful appearance in London each year from one to eight years old, her list being: First, as a yearling; sixth, as a two-year-old; second, as a three-year-old; first and reserve champion at four years old, five and seven; first in her class at six. She was not to be denied the absolute championship, however, and it fell to her in 1911. No Shire in history has achieved greater distinction than this, not even Honest Tom 1105, who won first prize at the Royal Show six years in succession, as the competition in those far-off days was much less keen than that which Pailton Sorais had to face, and it should be mentioned that she was also a good breeder, the foal by her side when she was sold made 310 guineas and another daughter 400 guineas.

Such are the kind of Shire mares that farmers want. Those that will work, win, and breed. As we have seen in this incomplete review, Aurea won the championship of the London show, together with her son. Belle Cole, the champion mare of 1908, bred a colt which realized 900 guineas as a yearling a few days before she herself gained her victory, a clear proof that showing and breeding are not incompatible.

CHAPTER XII

A Few Records

THE highest priced Shires sold by auction have already been given. So a few of the most notable sales may be mentioned, together with the dates they were held—

	£	s.	d.
Tring Park (draft), February 14, 1913: 32 Shires averaged	454	0	0
Tatton Park (dispersion), April 23, 1909: 21 Shires averaged	465	0	0
Tring Park (draft), February 14, 1905: 35 Shires averaged	266	15	0
The Hendre, Monmouth (draft), October 18, 1900: 42 Shires averaged	226	0	0
Sandringham (draft), February 11, 1898: 52 Shires averaged	224	7	9
Tring Park (draft), January 15, 1902: 40 Shires averaged	217	14	0
Tring Park (draft), January 12, 1898: 35 Shires averaged	209	18	2
Dunsmore (dispersion), February 11, 1909: 51 Shires averaged	200	12	0
Childwick (draft), February 13, 1901: 46 Shires averaged	200	0	0
Tandridge (dispersion), October 28, 1911: 84 Shires averaged	188	17	6

A FEW RECORDS

These ten are worthy of special mention, although there are several which come close up to the £200 average. That given first is the most noteworthy for the reason that Lord Rothschild only sold a portion of his stud, whereas the executors of the late Lord Egerton of Tatton sold their whole lot of twenty-one head, hence the higher average. Two clear records were, however, set up at the historical Tring Park sale in 1913, viz. the highest individual price for a stallion and the highest average price for animals by one sire, seven sons and daughters of Childwick Champion, making no less than £927 each, including two yearling colts.

The best average of the nineteenth century was that made at its close by the late Lord Llangattock, who had given a very high price privately for Prince Harold, by Harold, which, like his sire, was a very successful stock horse, his progeny making a splendid average at this celebrated sale. A spirited bidder at all of the important sales and a very successful exhibitor, Lord Llangattock did not succeed in winning either of the London Championships.

One private sale during 1900 is worth mentioning, which was that of Mr. James Eadie's two cup-winning geldings, Bardon Extraordinary and Barrow Farmer for 225 guineas each, a price which has only been equalled once to the writer's knowledge. This was in the autumn of 1910, when Messrs Truman gave 225 guineas for a gelding, at Messrs. Manley's Repository, Crewe, this specimen of the English lorry horse being bought for export to the United States.

In 1894 the late Lord Wantage held a sale which possessed unique features in that fifty animals catalogued were all sired by the dual London Champion and Windsor Royal (Jubilee Show) Gold Medal Winner, Prince William, to whom reference has already been made. The average was just over £116. As a great supporter of the old English breed, Lord Wantage, K.C.B., a Crimean veteran, deserves to be bracketed with the recently deceased Sir Walter Gilbey, inasmuch as that in 1890 he gave the Lockinge Cup for the best Shire mare exhibited at the London show, which Starlight succeeded in winning outright for Mr. Fred Crisp in 1892.

A FEW RECORDS

Sir Walter Gilbey gave the Elsenham Cup for the best stallion, value 100 guineas, in 1884, which, however, was not won permanently till the late Earl of Ellesmere gained his second championship with Vulcan in 1891. Since these dates the Shire Horse Society has continued to give the Challenge Cups both for the best stallion and mare.

The sales hitherto mentioned have been those of landowners, but it must not be supposed that tenant farmers have been unable to get Shires enough to call a home sale. On February 5, 1890, Mr. A. H. Clark sold fifty-one Shires at Moulton Eaugate, the average being £127 5s., the striking feature of this sale being the number of grey (Thumper) mares.

In February, 1901, Mr. Clark and Mr. F. W. Griffin, another very successful farmer breeder in the Fens, held a joint sale at Postland, the former's average being £100 6s. 9d., and the latter's £123 9s. 8d., each selling twenty-five animals.

The last home sale held by a farmer was that of Mr. Matthew Hubbard at Eaton, Grantham, on November 1, 1912, when an average of £73 was obtained for fifty-seven lots.

Reference has already been made to Harold, Premier, and Prince William, as sires, but there have been others equally famous since the Shire Horse Society has been in existence. Among them may be mentioned Bar None, who won at the 1882 London Show for the late Mr. James Forshaw, stood for service at his celebrated Carlton Stud Farm for a dozen seasons, and is credited with having sired over a thousand foals. They were conspicuous for flat bone and silky feather, when round cannon bones and curly hair were much more common than they are to-day, therefore both males and females by Bar None were highly prized; £2000 was refused for at least one of his sons, while a two-year-old daughter made 800 guineas in 1891. For several years the two sires of Mr. A. C. Duncombe, at Calwich, Harold and Premier, sired many winners, and in those days the Ashbourne Foal Show was worth a journey to see.

In 1899 Sir P. Albert Muntz took first prize in London with a big-limbed yearling, Dunsmore Jameson, who turned out to be the sire of strapping yearlings, two- and three-year-olds, which carried all before them in the show ring for several years, and a three-year-old son made the highest price ever realized at any of the Dunsmore Sales, when the stud was dispersed in 1909. This was 1025 guineas given by Lord Middleton for Dunsmore Jameson II. For four years in succession, 1903 to 1906, Dunsmore Jameson sired the highest number of winners, not only in London, but at all the principal shows. His service fee was fifteen guineas to "approved mares only," a high figure for a horse which had only won at the Shire Horse Show as a yearling. Among others he sired Dunsmore Raider, who in turn begot Dunsmore Chessie, Champion mare at the London Shows of 1912 and 1913. Jameson contained the blood of Lincolnshire Lad on both sides of his pedigree. By the 1907 show another sire had come to the front, and his success was phenomenal; this was Lockinge Forest King, bred by the late Lord Wantage in 1889, purchased by the late Mr. J. P. Cross, of Catthorpe Towers, Rugby, who won first prize, and reserve for the junior cup with him in London as a three-year-old, also first and

G

champion at the (Carlisle) Royal Show the same year, 1902. It is worth while to study the breeding of Lockinge Forest King.

Sire—Lockinge Manners.
Grand sire—Prince Harold.
Great grand sire—Harold.
Great great grand sire—Lincolnshire Lad II. 1365.
Great great great grand sire—Lincolnshire Lad 1196 (Drew's).

The dam of Lockinge Forest King was The Forest Queen (by Royal Albert, 1885, a great sire in his day); she was first prize winner at the Royal Show, Nottingham, 1888, first and champion, Peterborough, 1888, first Bath and West, 1887 and 1888, and numerous other prizes. Her dam traced back to (Dack's) Matchless (1509), a horse which no less an authority than the late Mr. James Forshaw described as "the sire of all time."

This accounts for the marvellous success of Lockinge Forest King as a stud horse, although his success, unlike Jameson's, came rather late in his life of ten years. He died in 1909. We have already seen that he has sired the highest priced Shire mare publicly sold. At the Newcastle Royal of 1908, both of the gold medal winners were by him, so were the two champions at the 1909 Shire Horse Show. His most illustrious family was bred by a tenant farmer, Mr. John Bradley, Halstead, Tilton, Leicester. The eldest member is Halstead Royal Duke, the London Champion of 1909, Halstead Blue Blood, 3rd in London, 1910, both owned by Lord Rothschild, and Halstead Royal Duchess, who won the junior cup in London for her breeder in 1912. The dam of the trio is Halstead Duchess III by Menestrel, by Hitchin Conqueror (London Champion, 1890).

Two other matrons deserve to be mentioned, as they will always shine in the history of the Shire breed. One is Lockington Beauty by Champion 457, who died at a good old age at Batsford Park, having produced Prince William, the champion referred to more than once in these pages, his sire being William the Conqueror. Then Marmion II (by Harold), who was first in London in 1891, and realized 1400 guineas at Mr. Arkwright's sale. Also a daughter, Blue Ruin, which won at London Show of 1889 for Mr. R. N. Sutton-Nelthorpe, but, unfortunately, died from foaling in that year. Another famous son was Mars

Victor, a horse of great size, and also a London winner, on more than one occasion. He was purchased by Mr. (Sir) Walter Gilbey from Mr. Freeman-Mitford (Lord Redesdale) in the year of his sire's—Hitchin Conqueror's—championship in 1890, for the sum of £1500. Another was Momus by Laughing Stock. Blue Ruin was own sister to Prince William, but the other three were by different sires.

To look at—I saw her in 1890—Lockington Beauty was quite a common mare with obviously small knees, and none too much weight and width, her distinguishing feature being a mane of extraordinary length.

The remaining dam to be mentioned as a great breeder is Nellie Blacklegs by Bestwick's Prince, famous for having bred five sons—which were all serving mares in the year 1891—and a daughter, all by Premier. The first was Northwood, a horse used long and successfully by Lord Middleton and the sire of Birdsall Darling, the dam of Birdsall Menestrel, London champion of 1904. The second, Hydrometer, first in London in 1889, then sold to the late Duke of Marlborough, and purchased when his stud was dispersed

A FEW RECORDS

in 1893 by the Warwick Shire Horse Society for 600 guineas. Then came Chancellor, sold at Mr. A. C. Duncombe's sale in 1891 for 1100 guineas, a record in those days, to Mr. F. Crisp, who let him to the Peterborough Society in 1892 for £500. Calwich Topsman, another son, realized 500 guineas when sold, and Senator made 350. The daughter, rightly named "Sensible," bred Mr. John Smith of Ellastone, Ashbourne, a colt foal by Harold in 1893, which turned out to be Markeaton Royal Harold, the champion stallion of 1897. This chapter was headed "A few records," and surely this set up by Premier and Nellie Blacklegs is one.

The record show of the Shire Horse Society, as regards the number of entries, was that of 1904, with a total of 862; the next for size was the 1902 meeting when 860 were catalogued. Of course the smallest show was the initial one of 1880, when 76 stallions and 34 mares made a total of 110 entries. The highest figure yet made in the public auction sales held at the London Show is 1175 guineas given by Mr. R. Heath, Biddulph Grange, Staffs., in 1911 for Rickford Coming

King, a three-year-old bred by the late Lord Winterstoke, and sold by his executors, after having won fourth in his class, although first and reserve for the junior cup as a two-year-old. He was sired by Ravenspur, with which King Edward won first prize in London, 1906, his price of 825 guineas to Lord Winterstoke at the Wolferton Sale of February 8, 1907, being the highest at any sale of that year. The lesson to be learned is that if you want to create a record with Shires you must begin and continue with well-bred ones, or you will never reach the desired end.

CHAPTER XIII

Judges at the London Shows, 1890-1915

The following are the Judges of a quarter of a century's Shires in London:—

1890. Clark, A. H., Moulton Eaugate, Spalding, Lincs.
Chapman, George, Radley, Hungerford, Berks.
Morton, John, West Rudham, Swaffham, Norfolk.
Nix, John, Alfreton, Derbyshire.

1891. Blundell, Peter, Ream Hills, Weeton Kirkham, Lancs.
Hill, Joseph B., Smethwick Hall, Congleton, Cheshire.
Morton, Joseph, Stow, Downham Market, Norfolk.
Smith, Henry, The Grove, Cropwell Butler, Notts.

1892. Heaton, Captain, Worsley, Manchester.
Morton, John, West Rudham, Swaffham, Norfolk.
Nix, John, Alfreton, Derbyshire.
Rowland, John W., Fishtoft, Boston, Lincs.

1893. Byron, A. W., Duckmanton Lodge, Chesterfield, Derbyshire.
Crowther, James F., Knowl Grove, Mirfield, Yorks.
Douglas, C. I., 34, Dalebury Road, Upper Tooting, London.
Smith, Henry, The Grove, Cropwell Butler, Notts.

1894. Heaton, Captain, Worsley, Manchester.
Chamberlain, C. R., Riddings Farm, Alfreton, Derbyshire.
Tindall, C. W., Brocklesby Park, Lincs.
Rowland, John W., Fishtoft, Boston, Lincs.

1895. Clark, A. H., Moulton Eaugate, Spalding, Lincs.
Freshney, T. B., South Somercotes, Louth, Lincs.
Rowell, John, Manor Farm, Bury, Huntingdon.
Smith, Henry, The Grove, Cropwell Butler, Notts.

1896. Green, Edward, The Moors, Welshpool.
Potter, W. H., Barberry House, Ullesthorpe, Rugby.
Rowland, John W., Fishtoft, Boston, Lincs.

1897. Chamberlain, C. R., Riddings Farm, Alfreton, Derbyshire.
Lewis, John, Trwstllewelyn, Garthmyl, Mont.
Wainwright, Joseph, Corbar, Buxton, Derbyshire.

1898. Clark, A. H., Moulton Eaugate, Spalding, Lincs.
Freshney, T. B., South Somercotes, Louth, Lincs.
Richardson, Wm., London Road, Chatteris, Cambs.

1899. Green, Edward, The Moors, Welshpool.
Griffin, F. W., Borough Fen, Peterborough.
Welch, William, North Rauceby, Grantham, Lincs.

1900. Clark, A. H., Moulton Eaugate, Spalding, Lincs.
Forshaw, James, Carlton-on-Trent, Newark, Notts.
Paisley, Joseph, Waresley, Sandy, Beds.

1901. Eadie, J. T. C., Barrow Hall, Derby.
Heaton, Captain, Worsley, Manchester.
Freshney, T. B., South Somercotes, Louth, Lincs.

1902. Clark, A. H., Moulton Eaugate, Spalding, Lincs.
Griffin, F. W., Borough Fen, Peterborough.
Rowell, John, Manor Farm, Bury, Huntingdon.

JUDGES AT LONDON SHOWS

1903. Nix, John, Alfreton, Derbyshire.
Richardson, William, Eastmoor House, Doddington, Cambs.
Grimes, Joseph, Highfield, Palterton, Chesterfield, Derbyshire.

1904. Freshney, T. B., South Somercotes, Louth, Lincs.
Smith, Henry, The Grove, Cropwell Butler, Notts
Whinnerah, James, Warton Hall, Carnforth, Lancs.

1905. Clark, A. H., Moulton Eaugate, Spalding, Lincs.
Blundell, John, Ream Hills, Weeton Kirkham, Lancs.
Green, Edward, The Moors, Welshpool.

1906. Eadie, J. T. C., The Knowle, Hazelwood, Derby.
Rowell, John, Bury, Huntingdon.
Green, Thomas, The Bank, Pool Quay, Welshpool.

1907. Griffin, F. W., Borough Fen, Peterborough.
Paisley, Joseph, Moresby House, Whitehaven.
Whinnerah, Edward, Warton Hall, Carnforth, Lancs.

1908. Clark, A. H., Moulton Eaugate, Spalding, Lincs.
Blundell, John, Lower Burrow, Scotforth, Lancs.
Howkins, W., Hillmorton Grounds, Rugby.

1909. Eadie, J. T. C., The Rock, Newton Solney, Burton-on-Trent.
Rowell, John, Bury, Huntingdon.
Thompson, W., jun., Desford, Leicester.

1910. Blundell, John, Lower Burrow, Scotforth, Lancs.
Cowing, G., Yatesbury, Calne, Wilts.
Green, Edward, The Moors, Welshpool.

1911. Green, Thomas, The Bank, Pool Quay, Welshpool.
Gould, James, Crouchley Lymm, Cheshire.
Measures, John, Dunsby, Bourne, Lincs.

1912. Clark, A. H., Moulton Eaugate, Spalding, Lincs.
Flowers, A. J., Beachendon, Aylesbury, Bucks.
Whinnerah, Edward Warton, Cranforth, Lancs.

1913 Blundell, John, Lower Burrow, Scotforth, Lancs.
Betts, E. W., Babingley, King's Lynn, Norfolk.
Griffin, F. W., Borough Fen, Peterborough.

1914 Forshaw, Thomas, Carlton-on-Trent, Newark, Notts.
Keene, R. H., Westfield, Medmenham, Marlow, Bucks.
Thompson, William, jun., Kibworth Beauchamp, Leicester.

1915 Eadie, J. T. C., Newton Solney, Burton-on-Trent.
Green, Edward, The Moors, Welshpool.
Mackereth, Henry Whittington, Kirkby Londsdale, Lancs.

This list is interesting for the reason that those who have awarded the prizes at the Shire Horse Show have, to a great extent, fixed the type to find favour at other important shows. Very often the same judges have officiated at several important exhibitions during the same season, which has tended towards uniformity in prize-winning Shires. On looking down the list, it will be seen that four judges were appointed till 1895, while the custom of the Society to get its Council from as many counties as possible has not been followed in the matter of judges' selection. For instance, Warwickshire—a great county for Shire breed-

JUDGES AT LONDON SHOWS 91

ing—has only provided two judges in twenty-six years, and one of them—Mr. Potter—had recently come from Lockington Grounds, Derby, where he bred the renowned Prince William. For many years Hertfordshire has provided a string of winners, yet no judge has hailed from that county, or from Surrey, which contains quite a number of breeders of Shire horses. No fault whatever is being found with the way the judging has been carried out. It is no light task, and nobody but an expert could, or should, undertake it; but it is only fair to point out that high-class Shires are, and have been, bred in Cornwall, and Devonshire, Kent, and every other county, while the entries at the show of 1914 included a stallion bred in the Isle of Man.

In 1890, as elsewhere stated, the membership of the Society was 1615, whereas the number of members given in the 1914 volume of the Stud Book is 4200. The aim of each and all is "to improve the Old English breed of Cart Horses," many of which may now be truthfully described by their old title of "War Horses."

CHAPTER XIV

THE EXPORT TRADE

AMONG the first to recognize the enormous power and possibilities of the Shire were the Americans. Very few London shows had been held before they were looking out for fully-registered specimens to take across the Atlantic. Towards the close of the 'eighties a great export trade was done, the climax being reached in 1889, when the Shire Horse Society granted 1264 export certificates. A society to safeguard the interests of the breed was formed in America, these being the remarks of Mr. A. Galbraith (President of the American Shire Horse Society) in his introductory essay: "At no time in the history of the breed have first-class animals been so valuable as now, the praiseworthy endeavour to secure the best specimens of the breed having the natural effect of enhancing prices all round. Breeders of Shire horses both in England and America have a hopeful and brilliant future before them, and by exercising good judgment in their selections, and giving due regard to pedigree and soundness, as well as individual merit, they will not only reap a rich pecuniary reward, but prove a blessing and a benefit to this country."

From the day that the Shire Horse Society was incorporated, on June 3, 1878, until now, America has been Britain's best overseas customer for Shire horses, a good second being our own colony, the Dominion of Canada. Another stockbreeding country to make an early discovery of the merits of "The Great Horse" was Argentina, to which destination many good Shires have gone. In 1906 the number given in the Stud Book was 118. So much importance is attached to the breed both in the United States and in the Argentine Republic that English judges have travelled to each of those country's shows to award the prizes in the Shire Classes.

Another great country with which a good and growing trade has been done is Russia. In 1904 the number was eleven, in 1913 it had increased to fifty-two, so there is evidently a market there which is certain to be extended when peace has been restored and our powerful ally sets about the stupendous, if peaceful, task of replenishing her horse stock.

Our other allies have their own breeds of draught horses, therefore they have not been customers for Shires, but with war raging in their breeding grounds, the numbers must necessarily be reduced almost to extinction, consequently the help of the Shire may be sought for building up their breeds in days to come.

German buyers have not fancied Shire horses to any extent—British-bred re-mounts have been more in their line.

In 1905, however, Germany was the destination of thirty-one. By 1910 the number had declined to eleven, and in 1913 to three, therefore, if the export of trade in Shires to "The Fatherland" is altogether lost, English breeders will scarcely feel it.

Australia, New Zealand, and South Africa are parts of the British Empire to which Shires have been shipped for several years. Substantial prizes in the shape of Cups and Medals are now given by the Shire Horse

Society to the best specimens of the breed exhibited at Foreign and Colonial Shows.

Encouraging the Export of Shires

The following is reprinted from the " Farmer and Stockbreeder Year Book" for 1906, and was written by S. H. L. (J. A. Frost):—

" The Old English breed of cart horse, or 'Shire,' is universally admitted to be the best and most valuable animal for draught purposes in the world, and a visitor from America, Mr. Morrow, of the United States Department of Agriculture, speaking at Mr. John Rowell's sale of Shires in 1889, said, 'Great as had been the business done in Shire horses in America, the trade is but in its infancy, for the more Shire horses became known, and the more they came into competition with other breeds, the more their merits for all heavy draught purposes were appreciated.'

"These remarks are true to-day, for although sixteen years have elapsed since they were made (1906), the massive Shire has more than held his own, but in the interests of the breed, and of the nearly four thousand members of the Shire Horse Society, it is still doubtful whether the true worth of the Shire horse is properly known and appreciated in foreign countries and towns needing heavy horses, and whether the export trade in this essentially British breed is not capable of further development. The number of export certificates granted by the Shire Horse Society in 1889 was 1264, which takes a good deal of beating, but it must be remembered that since then Shire horse breeding at home has progressed by leaps and bounds, and tenant farmers, who could only look on in those days, are now members of the flourishing Shire Horse Society and owners of breeding studs, and such prices as 800 guineas for a two-year-old filly and 230 guineas for a nine-months-old colt, are less frequently obtainable than they were then; therefore, an increase in the demand from other countries would find more Shire breeders ready to supply it, although up to the present the home demand has been and is very good, and weighty geldings continue to be scarce and dear."

The Number Exported

"It may be true that the number of horses exported during the last year or two has been higher than ever, but when the average value of those that go to 'other countries' than

Holland, Belgium, and France, is worked out, it does not allow of such specimens as would excite the admiration of a foreign merchant or Colonial farmer being exported, except in very isolated instances; then the tendency of American buyers is to give preference to stallions which are on the quality rather than on the weighty side, and as the mares to which they are eventually put are also light boned, the typical English dray horse is not produced.

"During the past year (1905) foreign buyers have been giving very high prices for Shorthorn cattle, and if they would buy in the same spirited manner at the Shire sales, a much more creditable animal could be obtained for shipment. As an advertisement for the Shire it is obviously beneficial that the Shire Horse Society—which is unquestionably the most successful breed society in existence—gives prizes for breeding stock and also geldings at a few of the most important horse shows in the United States. This tends to bring the breed into prominence abroad, and it is certain that many Colonial farmers would rejoice at being able to breed working geldings of a similar type to those which may be seen shunting trucks on any large railway station in England, or walking smartly along in front of a binder in harvest. The writer has a relative farming in the North-West Territory of Canada, and his last letter says, 'The only thing in the stock line that there is much money in now is horses; they are keeping high, and seem likely to for years, as so many new settlers are coming in all the time, and others do not seem able to raise enough for their own needs'; and it may be mentioned that almost the only kind of stallions available there are of the Percheron breed, which is certainly not calculated to improve the size, or substance, of the native draught horse stock.

The Cost of Shipping

"The cost of shipping a horse from Liverpool to New York is about £11, which is not prohibitive for such an indispensable animal as the Shire horse, and if such specimens of the breed as the medal winners at shows like Peterborough could be exhibited in the draught horse classes at the best horse shows of America, it is more than probable that at least some of the visitors would be impressed with their appearance, and an increase in the export trade in Shires might thereby be brought about.

"A few years ago the price of high-class Shire stallions ran upwards of a thousand pounds, which placed them beyond the reach of exporters; but the reign of what may be called 'fancy' prices appears to be over, at least for a time, seeing that the general sale averages have declined since that of Lord Llangattock in October, 1900, when the record average of £226 1s. 8d. was made, although the best general average for the sales of any single year was obtained in 1901, viz. £112 5s. 10d. for 633 animals, and it was during that year that the highest price for Shires was obtained at an auction sale, the sum being 1550 guineas, given by Mr. Leopold Salomons, for the stallion Hendre Champion, at the late Mr. Crisp's sale at Girton. Other high-priced stallions purchased by auction include Marmion II., 1400 guineas, and Chancellor, 1100 guineas, both by Mr. Crisp. Waresley Premier Duke, 1100 guineas, and Hendre Crown Prince, 1100 guineas, were two purchases of Mr. Victor Cavendish in the year 1897. These figures show that the worth of a really good Shire stallion can hardly be estimated, and it is certain that the market for this particular class of animal is by no means glutted, but rather the reverse, as the number of males offered at the stud sales is always limited, which proves that there is 'room on the top' for the stallion breeder, and with this fact in view and the possible chance of an increased foreign trade in stallions it behoves British breeders of Shires to see to it that there is no falling off in the standard of the horses 'raised,' to use the American word, but rather that a continual improvement is aimed at, so that visitors from horse-breeding countries may find what they want if they come to 'the stud farm of the world.'

"The need to keep to the right lines and breed from good old stock which has produced real stock-getting stallions cannot be too strongly emphasised, for the reason that there is a possibility of the British market being overstocked with females, with a corresponding dearth of males, both stallions and geldings, and although this is a matter which breeders cannot control they can at least patronise a strain of blood famous for its males. The group of Premier—Nellie Blacklegs' brothers, Northwood, Hydrometer, Senator, and Calwich Topsman—may be quoted as showing the advisability of continuing to use the same horse year after year if colt foals are bred, and wanted, and the sire is a horse of merit.

"With the number of breeders of Shire horses and the plentiful supply of mares, together with the facilities offered by local stallion-hiring societies, it ought not to be impossible to breed enough high-grade sires to meet the home demand and leave a surplus for export as well, and the latter of the class that will speak for themselves in other countries, and lead to enquiries for more of the same sort.

Few High Prices from Exporters

"It is noteworthy that few, if any, of the high prices obtained for Shires at public sales have come from exporters or buyers from abroad, but from lovers of the heavy breed in England, who have been either forming or replenishing studs, therefore, 'the almighty dollar' has not been responsible for the figures above quoted. Still it is probable that with the opening up of the agricultural industry in Western Canada, South Africa, and elsewhere, Shire stallions will be needed to help the Colonial settlers to build up a breed of horses which will be useful for both tillage and haulage purposes.

"The adaptability of the Shire horse to climate and country is well known, and it is satisfactory for home breeders to hear that Mr. Martinez de Hoz has recently sold ten Shires, bred in Argentina, at an average of

£223 2s. 6d., one, a three-year-old, making £525.

"Meanwhile it might be a good investment if a syndicate of British breeders placed a group of typical Shire horses in a few of the biggest fairs or shows in countries where weighty horses are wanted, and thus further the interests of the Shire abroad, and assist in developing the export trade."

It may be added that during the summer of 1906, H.M. King Edward and Lord Rothschild sent a consignment of Shires to the United States of America for exhibition.

CHAPTER XV

Prominent Present-Day Studs

SEEING that Lord Rothschild has won the greatest number of challenge cups and holds the record for having made the highest price, his name is mentioned first among owners of famous studs.

He joined the Shire Horse Society in February, 1891, and at the show of 1892 made five entries for the London Show at which he purchased the second prize three-year-old stallion Carbonite (by Carbon by Lincolnshire Lad II.) from Mr. Edward Green for 1100 guineas. He is remembered by the writer as being a wide and weighty horse on short legs which carried long hair in attendance, and this type has been found at Tring Park ever since. In 1895 his lordship won first and third with two chestnut fillies — Vulcan's Flower by the Champion Vulcan and Walkern Primrose by Hitchin Duke (by Bar None).

The former won the Filly Cup and was subsequently sold to help to found the famous stud of Sir Walpole Greenwell at Marden Park, Surrey, the sum given being a very high one for those days.

The first championship was obtained with the mare Alston Rose in 1901, which won like honours for Mr. R. W. Hudson in 1902, after costing him 750 guineas at the second sale at Tring Park, January 15, 1902.

Solace, bred by King Edward, was the next champion mare from Lord Rothschild's stud. Girton Charmer, winner of the Challenge Cup in 1905, was included in a select shipment of Shires sent to America (as models of the breed) by our late lamented King and Lord Rothschild in 1906. Princess Beryl, Belle Cole, Chiltern Maid, were mares to win highest honours for the stud, while a young mare which passed through Lord Rothschild's hands, and realized a four-figure sum for him as a two-year-old from the Devonshire enthusiasts, Messrs. W. and H. Whitley, is Lorna Doone, the Champion mare of 1914.

Champion's Goalkeeper, the Tring record-breaker, has been mentioned, so we can now refer to the successful stud of which he is the central figure, viz. that owned by Sir Walpole Greenwell at Marden Park, Woldingham, Surrey, who, as we have seen, bought a good filly from the Tring Stud in 1895, the year in which he became a member of the Shire Horse Society. At Lord Rothschild's first sale in 1898, he purchased Windley Lily for 430 guineas, and Moorish Maiden, a three-year-old filly, for 350, since when he has bid only for the best. At the Tandridge dispersion sale he gave over a thousand pounds for the Lockinge Forest King mare, Fuchsia of Tandridge, and her foal. Sir Walpole was one of the first to profit by the Lockinge Forest King blood, his filly, Marden Peach, by that sire having been a winner at the Royal of 1908, while her daughter, Marden Constance, has had a brilliant show career, so has Dunsmore Chessie, purchased from Mr. T. Ewart as a yearling, twice London Champion mare.

No sale has been held at Marden, but consignments have been sold at Peterborough, so that the prefix is frequently met with.

The stud owner who is willing to give £4305 for a two-year-old colt deserves success.

The Primley Stud

At the Dunsmore Sale on February 14, 1907, Mr. W. Whitley purchased Dunsmore Fuchsia (by Jameson), the London Cup winner of 1905 and 1906, for 520 guineas, also Quality by the same sire, and these two won second and third for him in London the same month, this being the first show at which the Primley shires took honours.

The purchase of Tatton Dray King, the Champion stallion of 1908, by Messrs. W. and H. Whitley in the spring of 1909 for 3700 guineas created quite a sensation, as it was an outstanding record, it stood so for nearly four years.

One of the most successful show mares in this—or any—stud is Mollington Movement by Lockinge Forest King, but the reigning queen is Lorna Doone, the London and Peterborough Champion of 1914, purchased privately from the Tring Park Stud. Another built on the same lines is Sussex Pride with which a Bucks tenant farmer, Mr. R. H. Keene, won first and reserve champion at the London Show of 1913, afterwards selling her to

Messrs. Whitley, who again won with her in 1914. With such animals as these Devonshire is likely to hold its own with Shires, although they do not come from the district known to the law makers of old as the breeding ground of "the Great Horse."

The Pendley Females

One of the most successful exhibitors of mares, fillies, and foals, at the shows of the past few seasons has been Mr. J. G. Williams, Pendley Manor, Tring. Like other exhibitors already mentioned, the one under notice owes much of his success to Lockinge Forest King. In 1908 Lord Egerton's Tatton May Queen was purchased for 420 guineas, she having been first in London as a yearling and two-year-old; Bardon Forest Princess, a reserve London Champion, and Barnfields Forest Queen, Cup winner there, made a splendid team of winners by the sire named. At the Tring Park sale of 1913 Mr. Williams gave the highest price made by a female, 825 guineas, for Halstead Duchess VII., by Redlynch Forest King. She won the Royal Championship at Bristol for him. One of the later acquisitions is Snelston Lady, by Slipton King, Cup winner and reserve Champion in London, 1914, as a three-year-old, first at the Royal, and reserve Champion at Peterborough. Mr. Williams joined the Shire Horse Society in 1906, since when he has won all but the London Championship with his mares and fillies.

A New Stud

After Champion's Goalkeeper was knocked down Mr. Beck announced that the disappointed bidder was Mr. C. R. H. Gresson, acting for the Edgcote Shorthorn Company, Wardington, Banbury, his date of admission to the Shire Horse Society being during that same month, February, 1913. Having failed to get the popular colt, his stable companion and half brother, Stockman III., was purchased for 540 guineas, and shown in London just after, where he won fourth prize. From this single entry in 1913 the foundation of the stud was so rapid that seven entries were made at the 1914 London Show. Fine Feathers was the first prize yearling filly, Blackthorn Betty the second prize two-year-old filly, the own bred

Edgcote Monarch being the second prize yearling colt. After the show Lord Rothschild's first prize two-year colt, Orfold Blue Blood, was bought, together with Normandy Jessie, the third prize yearling colt; so with these two, Fine Feathers, Betty, Chirkenhill Forest Queen, and Writtle Coming Queen, the Edgcote Shorthorn Co., Ltd., took a leading place at the shows of 1914. In future Edgcote promises to be as famous for its Shires as it has hitherto been for its Shorthorns.

Ducal Studs

A very successful exhibitor of the past season has been his Grace the Duke of Westminster, who owns a very good young sire in Eaton Nunsuch—so good that he has been hired by the Peterborough Society. Shires have been bred on the Eaton Hall estate for many years, and the stud contains many promising animals now.

Mention must be made of the great interest taken in Shires by the Duke of Devonshire who, as the Hon. Victor Cavendish, kept a first-class stud at Holker, Lancs. At the Royal Show of 1909 (Gloucester) Holker Mars was the Champion Shire stallion, Warton Draughtsman winning the Norwich Royal Championship, and also that of the London Show of 1912 for his popular owner.

Other Studs

Among those who have done much to promote the breeding of the Old English type of cart-horse, the name of Mr. Clement Keevil deserves a foremost place. At Blagdon, Malden, Surrey, he held a number of stud sales in the eighties and nineties, to which buyers went for massive-limbed Shires of the good old strains; those with a pedigree which traced back to Honest Tom (*alias* Little David), foaled in the year 1769, to Wiseman's Honest Tom, foaled in 1800, or to Samson a sire weighing 1 ton 8 cwt. Later he had a stud at Billington, Beds, where several sales were held, the last being in 1908, when Mr. Everard gave 860 guineas for the stallion, Lockinge Blagdon. Shortly before that he sold Blagdon Benefactor for 1000 guineas.

The prefix "Birdsall" has been seen in show catalogues for a number of years, which

PRESENT-DAY STUDS

mean that the animals holding it were bred, or owned, by Lord Middleton, at Birdsall, York, he being one of the first noblemen to found a stud, and he has ably filled the Presidential Chair of the Shire Horse Society. As long ago as the 1892 London Show there were two entries from Birdsall by. Lord Middleton's own sire, Northwood, to which reference is made elsewhere.

Another notable sire purchased by his lordship was Menestrel, first in London, 1900 (by Hitchin Conqueror), his most famous son being Birdsall Menestrel, dam Birdsall Darling by Northwood, sold to Lord Rothschild as a yearling. As a two-year-old this colt was Cup winner and reserve Champion, and at four he was Challenge Cup winner. A good bidder at Shire sales, the breeder of a champion, and a consistent supporter of the Shire breeding industry since 1883, it is regrettable that champion honours have not fallen to Lord Middleton himself.

Another stud, which was founded near Leeds, by Mr. A. Grandage, has now been removed to Cheshire. Joining the Shire Horse Society in 1892, his first entry in London was made in 1893, and four years later, in 1897, Queen of the Shires (by Harold) won the mare Championship for Mr. Grandage.

In 1909 the winning four-year-old stallion, Gaer Conqueror, of Lincolnshire Lad descent, was bought from Mr. Edward Green for 825 guineas, which proved to be a real good investment for Mr. Grandage, seeing that he won the championship of the Shire Horse Show for the two following years, 1910 and 1911.

Candidates from the Bramhope Stud, Monks Heath, Chelford, Cheshire, are likely to give a very good account of themselves in the days to come.

Among those who will have the best Shires is Sir Arthur Nicholson, Highfield, Leek, Staffs. His first London success was third prize with Rokeby Friar (by Harold) as a two-year-old in 1893, since which date he has taken a keen personal interest in the breeding of Shire horses, and has the honour of having purchased Pailton Sorais, the highest-priced mare yet sold by auction. At the Tring sale of 1913 he gave the second highest price of that day, viz., 1750 guineas for the three-year-

PRESENT-DAY STUDS

old stallion, Blacklands Kingmaker, who won first prize for him in London ten days after, but, alas, was taken ill during his season, for the Winslow Shire Horse Society, and died. Another bad loss to Sir Arthur and to Shire breeders generally was the death of Redlynch Forest King, seeing that he promised to rival his renowned sire, Lockinge Forest King, for begetting show animals.

Among the many good ones recently exhibited from the stud may be mentioned Leek Dorothy, twice first in London, and Leek Challenger, first as a yearling, second as a two-year-old, both of these being by Redlynch Forest King. With such as these coming on there is a future before the Shires of Sir Arthur Nicholson.

The name of Muntz is familiar to all Shire breeders owing to the fame achieved by the late Sir P. Albert Muntz. In 1899 Mr. F. E. Muntz, of Umberslade, Hockley Heath, Warwickshire, a nephew of the Dunsmore Baronet, joined the Shire Horse Society, and has since been President. Quite a good share of prizes have fallen to him, including the Cup for the best old stallion in London both in 1913 and

1914. The winner, Danesfield Stonewall, was reserved for the absolute championship on both occasions, and this typical "Old English Black" had a host of admirers, while Jones—the Umberslade stud groom—will never forget his parade before His Majesty King George at the 1913 show.

It used to be said that Shires did not flourish south of London, but Mr. Leopold Salomons, Norbury Park, Dorking, has helped to prove otherwise. Beginning with one entry at the 1899 Show, he has entered quite a string for several years, and the stud contains a number of high-class stallions, notably Norbury Menestrel, winner of many prizes, and a particularly well-bred and promising sire, and King of Tandridge (by Lockinge Forest King), purchased by Mr. Salomons at the Tandridge dispersion sale for 1600 guineas. At the sale during the London Show of 1914 Mr. Salomons realized the highest price with his own bred Norbury Coronation, by Norbury Menestrel, who, after winning third prize in his class, cost the Leigh Shire Horse Society 850 guineas, Norbury George, by the same sire, winning fifth prize, and making 600 guineas, both being three years old. This is the kind of advertisement for a stud, no matter where its situation.

Another Surrey enthusiast is Sir Edward Stern, Fan Court, Chertsey, who has been a member of the Shire Horse Society since 1903. He purchased Danesfield Stonewall from Mr. R. W. Hudson, and won several prizes before re-selling him to Mr. F. E. Muntz. His stud horses now includes Marathon II., champion at the Oxford County Show of 1910. Mares and fillies have also been successfully shown at the Royal Counties, and other meetings in the south of England from the Fan Court establishment.

A fine lot of Shires have been got together, at Tarnacre House, Garstang, and the first prize yearling at the London Show of 1914, King's Choice, was bred by Messrs. J. E. and A. W. Potter, who also won first with Monnow Drayman, the colt with which Mr. John Ferneyhough took first prize as a three-year-old. With stallions of his type and mares as wide, deep, and well-bred as Champion's Choice (by Childwick Champion), Shires full of character should be forthcoming from these Lancashire breeders.

The Carlton Stud continues to flourish, although its founder, the late Mr. James Forshaw, departed this life in 1908. His business abilities and keen judgment have been inherited by his sons, one of whom judged in London last year (1914), as his father did in 1900. This being a record in Shire Horse history for father and son to judge at the great Show of the breed.

Carlton has always been famous for its stallions. It has furnished London winners from the first, including the Champions Stroxton Tom (1902 and 1903), Present King II. (1906), and Stolen Duchess, the Challenge Cup winning mare of 1907.

The sires owned by the late Mr. Forshaw and his sons are too numerous to mention in detail. Bar None is spoken of elsewhere. Another very impressive stallion was What's Wanted, the sire of Mr. A. C. Duncombe's Premier (also mentioned in another chapter), and a large family of celebrated sons. His great grandsire was (Dack's) Matchless 1509, a great sire in the Fen country, which travelled through Moulton Eaugate for thirteen consecutive seasons. The late Mr. Forshaw's opinion of him is given on another page. One of the most successful Carlton sires of recent years has been Drayman XXIII., whose son, Tatton Dray King, won highest honours in London, and realized 3700 guineas when sold. Seeing that prizes were being won by stallions from this stud through several decades of last century, and that a large number have been travelled each season since, while a very large export trade has been done by Messrs. Forshaw and Sons, it need hardly be said that the influence of this stud has been world-wide.

It is impossible to mention all the existing studs in a little book like this, but three others will be now mentioned for the reason that they are carried on by those who formerly managed successful studs, therefore they have "kept the ball rolling," viz. that of Mr. Thomas Ewart, at Dunsmore, who made purchases on his own behalf when the stud of the late Sir P. A. Muntz—which he had managed for so long—was dispersed, and has since brought out many winners, the most famous of which is Dunsmore Chessie. Mr. R. H. Keene, under whose care the Shires of Mr. R. W. Hudson (Past-President of the Shire Horse

Society) at Danesfield attained to such prominence, although not actually taking over the prefix, took a large portion of the land, and carries on Shire breeding quite successfully on his own account.

The other of this class to be named is Mr. C. E. McKenna, who took over the Bardon stud from Mr. B. N. Everard when the latter decided to let the Leicestershire stud farm where Lockinge Forest King spent his last and worthiest years. Such enterprise gives farmers and men of moderate means faith in the great and growing industry of Shire Horse breeding.

Of stud owners who have climbed to prominence, although neither landowners, merchant princes, nor erstwhile stud managers, may be mentioned Mr. James Gould, Crouchley Lymm, Cheshire, whose Snowdon Menestrel was first in his class and reserve for the Stallion Cup at the 1914 London Show; Messrs. E. and J. Whinnerah, Warton, Carnforth, who won seventh prize with Warton Draughtsman in 1910, afterwards selling him to the Duke of Devonshire, who reached the top of the tree with him two years later.

Mr. Henry Mackereth, the new London judge of 1915, entered the exhibitors' list at the London Show of 1899. Perhaps his most notable horse is Lunesdale Kingmaker, with which Lord Rothschild won fourth prize in 1907, he being the sire of Messrs. Potter's King's Choice above mentioned.

Many other studs well meriting notice could be dealt with did time and space permit, including that of a tenant farmer who named one of his best colts "Sign of Riches," which must be regarded as an advertisement for the breed from a farmer's point of view.

Of past studs only one will be mentioned, that of the late Sir Walter Gilbey, the dispersal having taken place on January 13, 1915. The first Shire sale at Elsenham was held in 1885—thirty years ago—when the late Lord Wantage gave the highest price, 475 guineas, for Glow, by Spark, the average of £172 4s. 6d. being unbeaten till the Scawby sale of 1891 (which was £198 17s. 3d.).

Sir Walter has been mentioned as one of the founders of the Shire Horse Society; his services in aid of horse breeding were recognized by presenting him with his portrait in oils, the subscribers numbering 1250. The presentation was made by King Edward (then Prince of Wales) at the London Show of 1891.

CHAPTER XVI

THE FUTURE OUTLOOK

THIS book is written when war, and all that pertains to it, is the absorbing topic. In fact, no other will be listened to. What is the good of talking about such a peaceful occupation as that of agriculture while the nation is fighting for its very existence? To a certain extent this can be understood, but stock breeding, and more particularly horse breeding, cannot be suspended for two or three seasons and then resumed without causing a gap in the supply of horses coming along for future use.

The cry of the army authorities is for " more and more men," together with a demand for a constant supply of horses of many types, including the weight-moving War Horse, and if the supply is used up, with no provision being made for a quantity of four-footed recruits to haul the guns or baggage waggons in the days to come, the British Army, and most others, will be faced with a problem not easily solved.

The motor-mad mechanic may think that his chance has come, but generals who have to lead an army over water-logged plains, or snow-covered mountains, will demand horses, hitherto—and henceforth—indispensable for mounting soldiers on, rushing their guns quickly into position, or drawing their food supplies and munitions of war after them.

When the mechanic has provided horseless vehicles to do all this, horse breeding can be ignored by fighting men—not before. But horses, particularly draft horses, are needed for commercial use. So far, coal merchants are horse users, while brewers, millers, and other lorry users have not altogether discarded the horse-drawn vehicle.

For taking loads to and from the landing stage at Liverpool heavy horses will be in great demand after the war—perhaps greater than they have ever been. The railways will continue to exist, and, while they do, powerful Shire geldings must be employed; no other can put the necessary weight into the collar for shunting loaded trucks.

THE FUTURE OUTLOOK

During the autumn of 1914 no other kind of advice—although they got plenty of it—was so freely and so frequently given to farmers as this, "grow more wheat."

If this has been acted upon, and there is no doubt that it has, at least to some extent, it follows, as sure as the night follows the day, that more horses will be required by those who grow the wheat. The land has to be ploughed and cultivated, the crop drilled, cut, carted home and delivered to mill, or railway truck, all meaning horse labour.

It may happen that large farmers will use motor ploughs or steam waggons, but these are beyond the reach of the average English farmer. Moreover, when bought they depreciate in value, whether working or standing idle, which is exactly what the Shire gelding or brood mare does not do. If properly cared for and used they appreciate in value from the time they are put to work until they are six or seven years old, and by that age most farmers have sold their non-breeders to make room for younger animals. Horse power is therefore the cheapest and most satisfactory power for most farmers to use in front of field implements and farm waggons, a fact which is bound to tell in favour of the Shire in the coming times of peace which we anticipate.

When awarding prizes for the best managed farm, the judges appointed by the Royal Agricultural Society of England are instructed to consider—

"General Management with a view to profit," so that any breed of live stock which leaves a profit would help a competitor.

Only a short time ago a Warwickshire tenant farmer told his landlord that Shire horses had enabled himself and many others to attend the rent audit, "with a smile on his face and the rent in his pocket."

Most landlords are prepared to welcome a tenant in that state, therefore they should continue to encourage the industry as they have done during the past twenty-five years.

Wars come to an end—the "Thirty Years' War" did—so let us remember the Divine promise to Noah after the flood, "While the earth remaineth seedtime and harvest . . . shall not cease," Gen. 8 : 22. As long as there is sowing and reaping to be done horses—Shire horses—will be wanted.

THE FUTURE OUTLOOK

"Far back in the ages
　　The plough with wreaths was crowned,
The hands of kings and sages
　　Entwined the chaplet round;
Till men of spoil disdained the toil
　　By which the world was nourished,
And dews of blood enriched the soil
　　Where green their laurels flourished:
Now the world her fault repairs—
　　The guilt that stains her story;
And weeps; her crimes amid the cares
　　That formed her earliest glory.
The glory, earned in deadly fray,
　　Shall fade, decay and perish.
Honour waits, o'er all the Earth
　　Through endless generations,
The art that calls her harvests forth
　　And feeds the expectant nations."

INDEX

A

Alston Rose, champion mare 1901...104
Armour-clad warriors, 1, 7
Army horses, 6
Ashbourne Foal Show, 80
Attention to feet, 42
Aurea, champion mare, 18, 65
Author's Preface, v
Average prices, 76

B

Back breeding, value of, 11, 13, 39
Bakewell, Robert, 2, 22, 54
Bardon Extraordinary, champion gelding, 65, 78
Bardon Stud, 118
Bar None, 80
Bearwardcote Blaze, 60
Bedding, 35
Birdsall Menestrel, 84, 111
—— stud, 110
Black horses, Bakewell's, 55
Black horses from Flanders, 58
Blagdon Stud, 110
Blending Shire and Clydesdale breeds, 59
Boiled barley, 36
Bradley, Mr. John, 83
Bramhope stud, 111
Breeders, farmer, 27
Breeders, prizes for, 65
Breeding from fillies, 17
Breeding, time for, 31
Bury Victor Chief, champion in 1892...68, 69
Buscot Harold, champion stallion, 17, 65

C

Calwich Stud, 61, 80
Canada, 101
Carbonite, 103
Care of the feet, 42
Carlton Stud, 116
Cart-colts, 23
Cart-horses, 54
Castrating colts, 39
Certificate of Soundness, 62
Champion's Goalkeeper, champion in 1913 and 1914...67, 104
Champions bred at Sandringham, 3
Cheap sires, 12
Clark, Mr A H., 79
Clydesdales, 58
Coats of mail, 51
Coke's, Hon. E., dispersion sale, 3
Colonies, 94

INDEX

Colour, 38
Composition of food, 33
Condition and bloom, 36
Cost of feeding, 33
Cost of shipping Shires, 98
Crisp, Mr. F., 63, 70
Cross, Mr. J. P., 81
Crushed oats and bran, 31

D

Dack's Matchless, 82, 116
Danesfield Stonewall, 114
Details of shows, 60
Development grant, 14
Devonshire, Duke of, 109
Doubtful breeders, 37
Draught horses, 23
Drayman XXIII, 117
Drew, Lawrence, of Merryton, 59
Duncombe, Mr. A. C., 69, 80
Dunsmore Chessie, 81, 105
——— Gloaming, 3, 72
——— Jameson, 80
——— Stud, 80

E

Eadie, Mr. James, 65, 78
Early breeding, 17
Eaton Hall Stud, 109
Eaton Nunsuch, 109
Edgcote Shorthorn Company's Stud, 108
Effect of war on cost of feeding, 40
Egerton of Tatton, Lord, 2, 77
Ellesmere, Earl of, 2, 7, 70
Elsenham Cup, 18, 79
Elsenham Hall Stud, 119
English cart-horse, 2
Entries at London shows, 61
Everard, Mr. B. N., 118
Ewart, Mr. T., 117
Exercise, 23, 27
Export trade, 92, 95

F

Facts and figures, 61
Fattening horses, 26
Feet, care of, 42
Fillies, breeding from, 17
Flemish horses, 1, 53, 57
Flora, by Lincolnshire Lad, 60
Foals, time for, 31
Foals, treatment of, 32
Foods and feeding, 30
Formation of Shire Horse Society, 13
Forshaw, Mr. James, 80, 116
Foundation stock, 9
Founding a stud, 8
Freeman-Mitford, Mr., now Lord Redesdale, 62
Future outlook, 21

G

Gaer Conqueror, 112
Galbraith, Mr. A., 92
Geldings at the London Show, 64
———, demand for, 15, 24
———, production of, 15

INDEX

Gilbey, Sir Walter, 2, 14, 51, 54, 119
Girton Charmer, champion in 1905...104
Glow, famous mare, 16, 119
Good workers, 23
Gould, Mr. James, 118
Grading up, 8
Grandage, Mr. A., 111
Green, Mr. E., 112
Greenwell, Sir Walpole, 105
Griffin, Mr. F. W., 79

H

Halstead Duchess VII., 107
Halstead Royal Duke, champion in 1909...68, 83
Haltering, 28
Hamilton, Duke of, importatations, 58
Harold, 60
Hastings, Battle of, 53
Hay, 33
Heath, Mr. R., 85
Henderson's, Sir Alexander, successes in 1898...64
Hendre Champion, 99
Hendre Crown Prince, 70, 99
Hereditary diseases, 76
High prices, 69
Highfield Stud, Leek, 112
History of the Shire, 51
Hitchin Conqueror, London champion, 1891...62
Honest Tom, 74
Horse, population and the war, 18, 120
Horse-power cheapest, 123

Horses for the army, 6
Horses at Bannockburn, 52
How to show a Shire, 48
Hubbard, Mr. Matthew, 79
Huntingdon, Earl of, importations, 58

I

Importations from Flanders and Holland, 53, 57
Inherited complaints, 10

J

Judges at London Shire Shows, 1890–1915...87

K

Keene, Mr. R. H., 117
Keevil, Mr. Clement, 110
King Edward VII., 3, 73, 86, 102
King George, 114

L

Lady Victoria, Lord Wantage's prize filly, 17
Land suitable, 45
Landlords and Shire breeding, 3, 15
Langford Hall sale, 3
Leading, 28
Lessons in showing, 50
Letting out sires, 14
Lincolnshire Lad 1196...59
Linseed meal, 36

K

INDEX

Liverpool heavy horses 122
Llangattock, Lord, 5, 77
Local horse breeding societies, 15
Lockinge Cup, 78
Lockinge Forest King, 81
Lockington Beauty, 83
London Show, 61
Lorna Doone, 70, 104

M

McKenna, Mr. C. E., 118
Mackereth, Mr. H., 119
Management, 21, 23
Manger feeding, 33
Maple, Sir J. Blundell, 72
Marden Park Stud, 105
Mares, management of, 17
——, selection of, 8
Markeaton Royal Harold, 17, 60, 65
Marmion, 70
Mating, 20, 22
Members of Shire Horse Society, 63
Menestrel, 111
Michaelis, Mr. Max, 74
Middleton, Lord, 84, 110
Minnehaha, champion mare, 64
Mollington Movement, 106
Muntz, Mr. F. E., 113
Muntz, Sir P. Albert, 5, 72, 80

N

Nellie Blacklegs, 84
Nicholson, Sir Arthur, 74, 112
Norbury Menestrel, 114
Norbury Park Stud, 114
Numbers exported, 96

O

Oats, 33
Old English cart-horse, 2, 13, 51
—— —— war horse, 1, 50, 57
Origin and progress, 51
Outlook for the breed, 120
Over fattening, 26

P

Pailton Sorais, champion mare, 74, 112
Pedigrees, 8
Pendley Stud, 107
Ploughing, 2, 22, 57
Popular breed, a, 1
Potter, Messrs. J. E. and H. W., 115
Premier, 69, 84
Preparing fillies for mating, 18
Primley Stud, 106
Prince Harold, 77
Prince William, 69, 78
Prizes at Shire shows, 63
Prominent breeders, 103
—— Studs, 102
Prospects of the breed, 121

R

Rearing and feeding, 30
Records, a few, 77
Redlynch Forest King, 113

INDEX

Rent-paying horses, vi, 11, 124
Repository sales, 5
Registered sires, 13
Rickford Coming King, 85
Rock salt, 35
Rogers, Mr. A. C., 67
Rokeby Harold, champion in 1893 and 1895...60, 66, 68
Roman invasion, 51
Rothschild, Lord, 68, 102, 103
Rowell, Mr. John, 69, 95
Russia, 93

S

Sales noted, 4, 76
Salomons, Mr. Leopold, 99
Sandringham Stud, 3, 73, 86
Scawby sale, 63
Select shipment to U.S.A., 102
Selecting the dams, 9
Selection of mares, 8
—— of sires, 12
Separating colts and fillies, 39
Sheds, 35
Shire Horse Society, 2, 13, 91, 93
Shire or war horse, 1, 51
—— sales, 69, 76
Shires for war, 6, 121
—— as draught horses, 1
——, feeding, 30
—— feet, care of, 42
—— for farm work, 1, 22
—— for guns, 6
——, formation of society, 13, 93
——, judges, 81

Shires, London Show, 61
——, management, 12
——, origin and progress of, 51
—— pedigrees kept, 8
——, prices, 69, 76
——, prominent studs, 103
——, sales of, 76
——, showing, 48
——, weight of, 6
——, working, 25
Show condition, 26
Show, London, 60
Showing a Shire, 48
Sires, selection of, 12
Smith-Carington, Mr. H. H., 73
Solace, champion mare, 3
Soils suitable for horse breeding, 45
Soundness, importance of, 9
Spark, 69
Stallions, 12
Starlight, champion mare 1891... 62, 78
Stern, Sir E., 115
Street, Mr. Frederick, 2
Stroxton Tom, 116
Stud Book, 2, 13, 91
Stud, founding a, 8
Studs, present day, 103
—— sales, 4, 76
Stuffing show animals, 26, 37
Suitable foods and system of feeding, 30
Sutton-Nelthorpe, Mr. R. N., 63, 83
System of feeding, 30

INDEX

T

Tatton Dray King, 71
—— Herald, 71
Team work, 23
"The Great Horse," Sir Walter Gilbey's book, 14, 51, 54
Training for show, 48,
—— for work, 27
Treatment of foals, 32
Tring Park Stud, 4, 103
Two-year-old champion stallions, 67
Two-year-old fillies, 17

U

United States, Shires in the, 3, 92
Unsoundness, 10

V

Value of pedigrees, 8
—— of soundness, 10
Veterinary inspection, 62
Virlean, champion in 1891... 70, 79

W

Wantage, Lord, 2, 78
War demand, 121
War horse, vi, 51, 91
War and breeding, 18
Warton Draughtsman, 118
Wealthy stud-owners, 14
Weaning time, 33
Weight of Armoured Knight, 51
Weight of Shires, 6
Welshpool Shire Horse Society, 70
Westminster, Duke of, 109
What's Wanted, 116
Whinnerah, Messrs. E. and J., 118
Whitley, Messrs. W. and H., 106
Williams, Mr. J. G., 107
Wintering, 40
—— foals, 35
Winterstoke, Lord, 86
Work of Shire Horse Society, 13, 60
Working stallions, 25
World's war, v, 120
Worsley Stud, 7

Y

Yards, 35

THE END

VINTON & COMPANY, LTD., 8, BREAM'S BUILDINGS, CHANCERY LANE, LONDON, E.C.

BIBLIOLIFE

Old Books Deserve a New Life
www.bibliolife.com

Did you know that you can get most of our titles in our trademark **EasyScript**™ print format? **EasyScript**™ provides readers with a larger than average typeface, for a reading experience that's easier on the eyes.

Did you know that we have an ever-growing collection of books in many languages?

Order online:
www.bibliolife.com/store

Or to exclusively browse our **EasyScript**™ collection:
www.bibliogrande.com

At BiblioLife, we aim to make knowledge more accessible by making thousands of titles available to you – quickly and affordably.

Contact us:
BiblioLife
PO Box 21206
Charleston, SC 29413

Lightning Source UK Ltd.
Milton Keynes UK
UKOW010746111212

203468UK00011B/142/P